Ida Wirak Trettevik is the woman behind Witre Design, a knitting pattern company, which launched in 2018. The brand is all about creating patterns that will inspire others to knit their own wardrobe, piece by piece, using materials of the highest quality and longevity.

Ida has been knitting from a very young age, having learnt from her mother and aunt; but she found her true vocation in advanced knitting when she was ordered to rest while pregnant with one of her sons. She and her husband and their three boys now live on the Norwegian island of Engeløya.

Ida presently has over 82,000 followers on her Instagram account under the handle @witredesign

www.witredesign.no

Ida Wirak Trettevik

A Knitter's Year

30 modern knits for every season

Witre Design

Photography: Helena Krekling

SEARCH PRESS

A Knitter's Year is a book of knitting patterns that tells two stories in one. The stories emerge simultaneously, on each page, and are both equally important to the origin of this book.

Firstly, there is the story of handicraft, and my desire to develop designs and create knitting patterns as 'Witre Design' (Witre is a portmanteau of my name). It is about inspiring others to knit their own wardrobes with needles and yarn, all revolving around the concept of 'slow fashion'. The garments in the book are easy to wear through different seasons and are modern in design, inspired by today's fashions and street style. The aim is for the individual knitter to end up with a good quality, long-lasting wardrobe, especially designed for them.

The second story in *A Knitter's Year* is told through the pictures. The book was created over a whole year. A year of my life. From January with snow and winter in Oslo, Norway through spring, summer and an autumn in a completely different place. When this project began, it wasn't certain where my family and I were going to live. What did we need, really, to have a good life? For six years we had been living in the centre of Oslo. We had three children who all saw themselves as Oslo boys, and we loved living in a lively apartment block with friendly neighbours. Nevertheless, we wanted other things – more air, more countryside, more space to just be, and possibly the freedom that comes from being able to choose something completely different.

The pictures are taken in places where I have spent a lot of time. The people in them are people in my life. And the clothes are designed to be everyday garments you can wear frequently wherever you happen to be.

This year our summer was very different from usual. Because this summer we decided to move. We chose to move away from what we had in Oslo, from family and good friends. Sometimes you move because you have to, other times because you choose to. We chose. And there were lots of tears because we were really scared of having made the wrong choice, as the moving van drove northwards.

As I write this foreword, I'm sitting in a white-painted wooden house on the island of Engeløya in Nordland, in northern Norway. If I turn around and look out of the window on the other side of the room, I can see the sheer rock wall of the Lofoten islands stretching along the horizon. When we got here, the sun barely dipped below the mountain tops before it rose again. No wonder the boys thought they could get up far too early and we adults thought we could stay up far too late. But we have got used to it. The air is clear and fresh. The sand on the beach is completely white and it glitters like snow when you run out for a swim. We have even acquired two kittens, just to make life in the country right and proper. And we love living here. At the moment, we're most excited about seeing the Northern Lights for the first time as autumn will soon be here.

So this is where *A Knitter's Year* ends, in north Norway. I hope the pictures show the amazing contrast and beauty of city and rural living, and that you will like them. And that you will flick through them when you want to rest your eyes, or find the next garment you want to put time and thought into.

Ida

Foreword

Winter

GRÜNER MITTENS

Taking their name from an area of Oslo, the Grüner mittens have a narrow fit and an extra-long ribbed cuff. The pattern increases for the thumb as you go, ensuring a good fit over the whole hand. The mittens are chunky and warm, as the yarn has been chosen to make mittens that last.

Sizes:	S(M:L:XL)
Approx. width:	9(10:11.5:12)cm / 3½(4:4½:4¾)in
Suggested yarns:	Sandnes Børstet Alpakka and Sandnes Peer Gynt
Yarn amount:	1(1:1:1) ball of 50g/110m/120yd Børstet Alpakka, chunky (bulky); and 1(1:2:2) balls of 50g/91m/98yd balls of Peer Gynt, DK (8-ply/light worsted) yarn
Tension:	15 sts to 10cm (4in) in stocking (stockinette) st on 6mm (UK 4, US 10 needles)
Suggested needles:	6mm (UK 4, US 10) double-pointed needles, or circular needles using the magic loop method

---

Cast on 20 (20:22:24) sts loosely on 6mm (UK 4, US 10) needles using 1 strand of each yarn together. Work in the round in k1, p1 rib until work measures 9(9:10:10)cm / 3½(3½:4:4)in. Change to stocking (stockinette) st, place a marker at start of round and inc 3(5:6:6) sts evenly across first round. Cont working in the round in stocking (stockinette) st while increasing for thumb as foll:

Left mitten: *knit until 1 st before marker, m1 right. Work 1 round in stocking (stockinette) st*. Rep between * and * until you have increased 5(5:6:6) times in total. At the same time, move the st that you inc into 1 st to right each time as foll: work until 2 sts before marker, inc to right. Next round, work until 3 sts before marker, etc.

Right mitten: *k1, m1 left, knit to end of round. Work 1 round in stocking (stockinette) st*. Rep between * and * until you have increased 5(5:6:6) times in total. At the same time, move the st you inc into 1 st to left each time as foll: k2, inc to left. Next round, k3, inc to left, etc.

After the last increased st: work 1 round in stocking (stockinette) st, and place 6(6:7:7) sts on a st holder or waste yarn. These will be the new sts plus 1 extra st in towards palm. Cast on 6(6:7:7) sts behind thumb. You now have 28(30:34:36) sts on your needles. Cont in stocking (stockinette) st in the round until work measures 15(16:18:19)cm / 6(6¼:7:7½)in from end of rib. Place a new marker after 14(15:17:18) sts. The markers mark the sides of the mittens.

Cast (bind) off for top: on both front and back of mitten, first 2 sts after marker: k2tog tbl. Last 2 sts before next marker: k2tog. Cont until 2 sts rem on needles. If you end with an odd number of sts, k2tog tbl, place st back on left needle and slip st to the left over the st you just knitted. Break yarn, thread through rem sts and fasten off.

Thumb: place sts on needle and pick up 1 st in each cast (bound) off st for thumb. 12(12:14:14) sts. Place marker in each side. Knit in the round until thumb measures 5(5.5:6:6.5)cm / 2(2¼:2½:2¾)in or to desired length. Cast (bind) off thumb as described for 'Cast (bind) off for top' but stop when 6(6:8:8) sts rem, then k2tog all the way around. Break yarn, thread through rem sts and fasten off. Sew a couple of sts at base of thumb if there is a hole.

Weave in all loose ends.

#grünervotter
#grünermittens
#witredesign

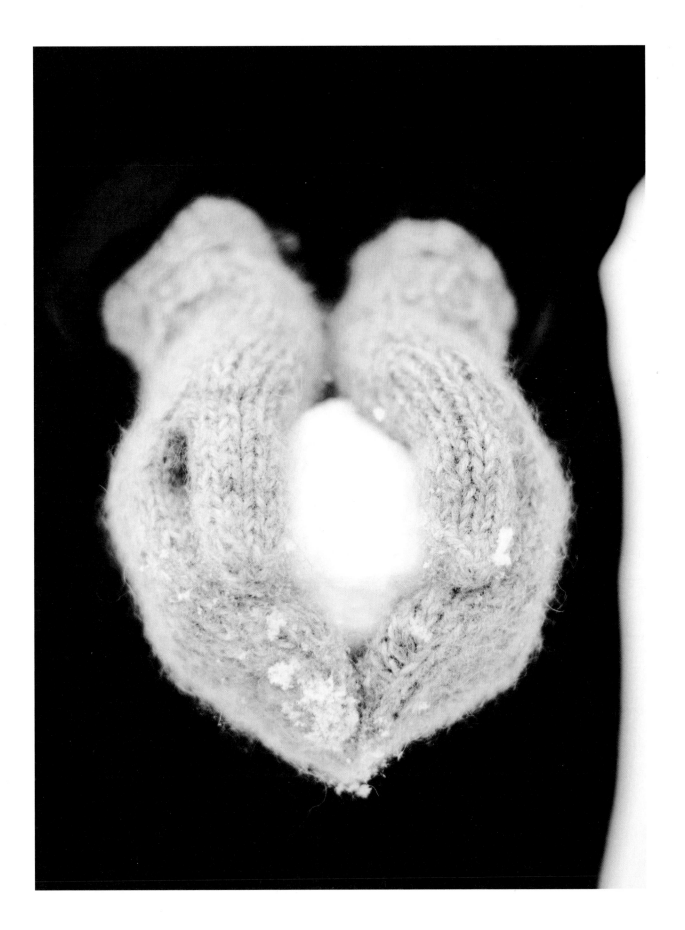

GRÜNER BEANIE

The Grüner beanie is knitted using two strands of yarn on big needles for a cool, chunky look. Its extra-long brim means it sits well, covering your whole head, and is really warm. The combination of yarns was chosen to make a hat that would stand the test of time.

See Grüner beanie with ear flaps on page 43.

Sizes:	Age 1–2 (3–7:8–12:adult:large adult)
Approx. hat circumference:	29(32:32:34:37)cm / 11½(12½:12½:13½:14½)in in rib
Suggested yarns:	Sandnes Peer Gynt and Sandnes Børstet Alpakka
Yarn amount:	(1:1:2:2:2) balls of 50g/91m/98yd Peer Gynt, DK (8-ply/ light worsted); and (1:1:1:1:1) ball of 50g/110m/120yd Børstet Alpakka, chunky (bulky) yarn
Tension:	14 sts to 10cm (4in) square in rib
Suggested needles:	7mm (UK 2, US 10½/11) circular needle

Cast on 40(44:44:48:52) sts loosely on a 7mm (UK 2, US 10½/11) circular needle using 1 strand of each yarn together. Place marker at start of round. Work in the round in k1, p1 rib until work measures 31(35:38:39:40)cm / 12¼(13¾:15:15¼:15¾)in. On next round, *k3tog, p1*, rep between * and * to end of round. Work 2 rounds in rib patt as set. On next round, k2tog for whole round. Thread yarn through rem sts, pull together tightly and fasten off. Weave in all loose ends. Fold up the brim so the turn-up measures approx. 9(10:11:12:13)cm / 3½(4:4¼:4¾:5)in.

Ear flaps, for ages 1–2: Pick up for the ear flaps at back of hat with approx. 6cm (2¼in) between the flaps. Pick up 10 sts on the fold of the brim, from RS. Work 3 rows in stocking (stockinette) st. Cont working back and forth, decreasing as foll on RS rows: k2tog tbl, work to last 2 sts, k2tog. Cont until 2 sts rem. Make an i-cord 22cm (8¾in) long or desired length. Rep on other side.

Weave in all loose ends.

#grünerlua #grünerbeanie #witredesign

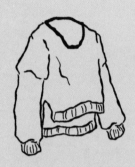

THICK WINTER SWEATER

This sweater is really thick and warm, and a gorgeous everyday sweater for cold winter days. Because, yes, clothes can be cool and practical, both at the same time. The sweater goes well with high-waisted trousers and skirts as it is shorter at the front than at the back. It is still warm and cozy, and the longer back keeps your bottom nice and warm. It is knitted from the bottom up, and the front and back sections are grafted together at the shoulders. Stitches are then picked up for the sleeves, which are knitted downwards to the desired length.

Sizes:	XS(S:M:L:XL)
Approx. measurements:	Chest: 100(110:120:130:140)cm /
	39½(43¼:47¼:51:55)in;
	Front length: 42(45:48:51:54)cm /
	16½(17¾:19:20:21¼)in;
	Back: approx. 10cm (4in) longer
Yarn amount:	14(16:18:20:22) balls of 50g/35m/38yd balls of super
	chunky (super bulky) yarn
Tension:	8 sts to 10cm (4in) square in stocking (stockinette) st
Suggested needles:	12mm (UK -, US 17) circular needle

Cast on 43(47:51:55:59) sts on a 12mm (UK -, US 17) circular needle. Working back and forth, work 8 rows in rib as foll: k1 (edge st), k1, p1 to end of row. End with k1 + 1 edge st. Work 8 rows in stocking (stockinette) st. Set work aside.

Rep between * and * for back. Work 16 rows in stocking (stockinette) st after end of rib. This makes the back longer than the front.

Now knit both front and back onto the same needle as foll: work until 3 sts rem on the needle you are using and place these 3 sts on a spare needle. Place the spare needle next to the needle for the front with sts for the back on top. Knit sts together in pairs, one from the spare needle and one from the other needle. This will ensure that the back overlaps the front at the split. Rep on the other side, placing the back on top here too. 80(88:96:104:112) sts. Place a marker in the centre st of the three sts merged together at each side. These mark the sides of the sweater, where the armholes will come later on.

Cont in stocking (stockinette) st in the round until work measures 24(26:28:30:32)cm / 9½(10¼:11:11¾:12½)in, measured from the front. Cast (bind) off 3 sts on each side, the marker st and 1 st each side of it.

Front: work back and forth in stocking (stockinette) st until work measures 31(33:35:37:39)cm / 12¼(13:13¾:14½:15¼)in measured from the front. On next RS row, cast (bind) off 3 sts at centre front. 17(19:21:23:25) sts on each side of ront.

Right side of front: working back and forth, at the end of each row at neck edge k2tog 5(6:6:7:7) times in total. Note: always slip first st on next row off loosely and work edge sts as knit sts on RS. Work until front measures 42(45:48:51:54)cm / 16½(17¾:19:20:21¼)in. Place sts on a holder or waste yarn.

Left side of front: starting at the armhole and working back and forth, k2tog at the end of each row at neck edge as described for 'Right side of front'. Remember to keep your edge sts looking neat. Place sts on a holder or waste yarn.

Back: work back and forth until back measures same length as front. Graft sts on back and front together for the best result. Or cast (bind) off and sew together at the shoulders. Leave rem sts for neck on needle and cast (bind) off neatly.

Sleeves: pick up 32(36:40:44:48) sts around armhole. Place marker at centre underarm. Working in the round, dec 1 st after first st and 1 st before last st every 6cm (2¼in), 5(6:6:7:7) times in total. Work until sleeve measures 36(38:40:42:44)cm / 14¼(15:15¾:16½:17¼)in or to desired length. Dec to 14(16:16:18:18) sts and work 8 rounds in k1, p1 rib. Cast (bind) off loosely.

Rep for other sleeve. Add a couple of sts at the neckline if necessary.

Weave in all loose ends.

#tjukkvintergenser
#thickwintersweater
#witredesign

Tips
• *All bodies are different. It is a good idea to measure the knitting against the wearer as you go along.*
• *Remember to check your tension.*
• *The stitches at the neck are not picked up for a neckband, so it is important that your edge stitches look good. Always slip first st off loosely and work edge sts as knit sts.*

CLASSY ZIP SKIRT

The classy zip skirt is a long, figure-hugging skirt that can be made with or without a zip. The skirt is knitted in Norwegian wool, making it very warm, and perfect for feeling well-dressed on cold winter days. The waist is fitted to the body with elastic inserted into a casing when the skirt is finished. Short rows are used at the back for a good fit. The pattern can be adjusted to make the skirt longer or shorter, and different-length zips can be used too.

Sizes:	XS(S:M:L)
Approx. measurements:	Width at widest point: 88(100:109:117)cm/ 34¾(39½:43:46)in;
	Length: 80cm (31½in) or to desired length
Suggested yarn:	Rauma Vams
Yarn amount:	6(7:8:9) balls of 50g/83m/91yd Rauma Vams, aran
	(10-ply/worsted) yarn
Tension:	14 sts to 10cm (4in) square in stocking (stockinette) st on
	6mm (UK 4, US 10) needles
Suggested needles:	5mm (UK 6, US 8) and 6mm (UK 4, US 10) circular needles
Approx. length of zip:	38cm (15in) or desired length
Extras:	Elastic, 3cm (1¼in) wide, and the circumference of your waist
	minus 5cm (2in); sewing needle and thread

Cast on 90(106:118:130) sts using a 5mm (UK 6, US 8) circular needle and work 4cm (1½in) in stocking (stockinette) st in the round. Purl 1 round and work another 4cm (1½in) in stocking (stockinette) st. Fold edge over and knit it down on next round, remembering to leave a gap of 2–3 sts at start of round to insert the elastic at the end. Or sew down this top casing once the skirt is finished, but remember that all foll measurements assume that the top 4cm (1½in) have been folded over and are measured from the fold line at the front.

Change to a 6mm (UK 4, US 10) circular needle and work 1 round in stocking (stockinette) st, while increasing 10 sts evenly across round. 100 (116) 128 (140) sts. Place marker at start of round (centre back), one marker at centre front and one at each side. There should be the same number of sts between each marker.

You are now going to work short rows to make the skirt slightly higher at the back. Work 12 sts past centre back marker. Turn and work 12 sts past centre back marker in the other direction. Continue as set, working 4 sts further past marker each time until you have turned four times on each side in total.

Cont in stocking (stockinette) st in the round. When work measures 12cm (4¾in) measured at the front, start to inc evenly at sides to make skirt wider. Inc 1 st after first st and 1 st before last st at side markers, 4 sts inc in total per round. Inc as set every 5cm (2in) six times in total. 124(140:152:164) sts. Cont in stocking (stockinette) st in the round until skirt measures 40cm (15¾in) measured from the front. Knit to centre front marker, turn and purl back to centre front marker. Continue to work back and forth to make a space for the zip until skirt measures 78cm (30¾in). Change to a 5mm (UK 6, US 8) needle and work 2cm (¾in) in rib as foll: k1 (edge st), k1, p1 and finish with k1 (edge st). Cast (bind) off in rib.

Zip: lay skirt flat on a table. Attach zip to split in skirt using pins to make sure it does not pucker as foll: place one pin at the bottom and at the top, in the middle and then in the middle of these pins. Rep until the zip is smooth and even all the way down, then rep on the other side. Try on the skirt before tacking the zip down with sewing thread. Sew the zip in by hand using yarn along the edge sts.

Insert a piece of elastic inside the casing at the top, cut to fit your own waist, then sew the opening closed.

Weave in all loose ends.

#classyzippskirt
#classyzipskirt
#witredesign

Tips

• *All bodies are different. It is a good idea to measure the knitting against the wearer as you go along.*

• *Remember to check your tension.*

• *Short rows are worked at the back. Search for videos on 'short rows' to see the technique in more detail.*

• *A casing for elastic is created at the waist. The edge can be knitted down as you go. If you want to try it out, search online for 'knit a casing'.*

• *The waist will feel too big before you have inserted the elastic.*

WOMEN'S URBAN POLAR SWEATER

The urban polar sweater is a soft, warm sweater, knitted using two strands of yarn on big needles. It works well in town, going to or from work, in the forest or out at sea. The neckband is doubled over in rib, making a snug and close-fitting neckline that is not too tight. The zip is practical but is also an eye-catching detail. The sweater is knitted from the bottom up. The zip is sewn in by hand with one strand of chunky (bulky) yarn. Stitches are picked up for the sleeves around the armhole and worked down to the length desired. The women's version is slimmer-fitting while the men's version is more of a unisex pattern.

• *All bodies are different. It is a good idea to measure the knitting against the wearer as you go along.*
• *Remember to check your tension.*
• *The sweater is grafted together at the shoulders. For more information, search online for videos on 'grafting stocking (stockinette) stitch' or 'Kitchener stitch'.*

Sizes:	XS(S:M:L:XL)
Approx. measurements:	Chest: 80(90:100:110:120)cm / 31½(35½:39½:43¼:47¼)in;
	Length: 60(63:66:69:72)cm / 23½(24¾:26:27¼:28¼)in
Suggested yarns:	Sandnes Peer Gynt and Sandnes Børstet Alpakka
Yarn amount:	6(7:8:8:9) balls of 50g/91m/98yd Peer Gynt, DK (8-ply/light worsted); and
	5(6:7:7:8) balls of 50g/110m/120yd Børstet Alpakka, chunky (bulky) yarn
Tension:	12 sts to 10cm (4in) square in stocking (stockinette) st on 7mm (UK 2, US 10½/11) needles
Suggested needles:	7mm (UK 2, US 10½/11) circular needle and 6mm (UK 4, US 10) circular needle for rib
Approx. length of zip:	23cm (9in). You can adapt the pattern to your chosen zip by a couple of centimetres (¾in) or so by making the neck higher or lower. It is not recommended to buy a zip that is a lot longer or shorter than the length stated.

Cast on 96(108:120:132:144) sts on a 6mm (UK 4, US 10) circular needle using 1 strand of each yarn together. Work 7 rounds of k1, p1 rib. Change to 7mm (UK 2, US, 10½/11) circular needle and stocking st. Place one marker at start of round and one at the halfway point. These mark the sides of the sweater and where you will later divide for the armhole. Work in stocking (stockinette) st until work measures 39(41:43:45:47)cm / 15¼(16¼:17:17¾:18½)in. Cast (bind) off 4 sts at each side, 2 before and 2 after marker.

Front: work back and forth across front until work measures 44(46:48:50:52)cm / 17¼(18:19:19¾:20½)in. Place marker at centre front, where zip will be inserted.

Left front: on next RS row, knit until 7 sts before marker. Work these sts in p1, k1 rib and end with k1 (edge st) before marker. Turn and work in patt as set. Rep until work measures 56(58:60:62:64)cm / 22(22¾:23¼:24½:25¼)in. Place the 7 sts at the neck (the rib sts) onto a st holder or waste yarn. Continue to work back and forth in stocking st. At the same time, on each RS row, knit to last 2 sts before neck edge, k2tog. Rep this dec 3(3:3:4:5) times in total. Work back and forth across rem sts until work measures 60(63:66:69:72)cm / 23½(24¾:26:27¼:28¼)in. Break yarn. Leave sts on needle or move to a st holder or thread.

Right front: starting at armhole, purl until 7 sts before marker. Work these sts in k1, p1 rib and end with k1 (edge st) before marker. Turn and work in patt as set. Rep until work measures 56(58:60:62:64)cm / 22(22¾:23¼:24½:25¼)in. Place the 7 sts at the neck, the rib sts, onto a st holder or waste yarn. Continue to work back and forth in stocking (stockinette) st. At the same time, on each WS row, purl to last 2 sts before neck edge, p2tog. Rep this dec 3(3:3:4:5) times in total. Work back and forth across rem sts until work measures 60(63:66:69:72)cm / 23½(24¾:26:27¼:28¼. Break yarn. Leave sts on needle or move to a st holder or waste yarn.

Back: work back and forth in stocking (stockinette) st until work measures 61(64:67:70:73)cm / 24(25¼:26½:27½:28¾)in, i.e. 1cm (½in) longer than the front. Graft sts on fronts to same number of sts on each side of back. Or cast (bind) off and sew together at shoulders. Leave rem sts for neck on needle.

Neck: knit sts for right front from holder/waste yarn onto a 6mm (UK 4, US 10) circular needle in rib patt as set. Pick up sts along neck edge and knit neck sts onto needle in stocking (stockinette) st. Pick up same number of sts along other side of neck. Knit sts on holder for left front onto needle in patt as set. Approx. 55(55:57:59:59) sts. Work back and forth in rib patt as set on front edges and continue rib patt around whole neck. Work back and forth in rib until neckband measures 22cm (8¾in) measured from back. Here you can knit the neck longer or shorter to fit your chosen zip. Remember that the neckband will be folded over, so check against the zip to make sure it will fit. Cast (bind) off loosely. Check as you cast (bind) off that the edges are stretchy enough.

Zip: fold the neckband to the inside then sew down by hand using yarn. Start approx. 1cm (½in) in on each side to make room for the zip afterwards. Then insert the zip between the layers of the neck on each side, and on down the inside of the opening. It should not go all the way up to the edge. Make sure you are happy with the zip placement. Start by pinning at the bottom and at the top, then in the middle of these pins. Make sure that the zip is sitting well and is even on both sides. Sew zip in by hand using 1 strand of chunky (bulky) yarn. The sts should be sewn inside the edge st and run all the way to the top and bottom of the zip for the best result.

Sleeves: pick up approx. 12 sts per 10cm (4in) around armhole – approx. 50(52:54:56:58) sts. Work in the round in stocking (stockinette) st and place a marker at centre underarm on first round. At the same time, k2tog after first st and k2tog before last st at each side of marker every 7 rounds. Work until sleeve measures 46(47:48:48:48)cm / 18(18½:19:19:19)in or to desired length and dec to 22(22:24:26:26) sts. Change to 6mm (UK 4, US 10) needle and work 7 rounds in k1, p1 rib. Cast (bind) off in rib. Rep for other sleeve.

Weave in all loose ends.

#urbanpolargenser #urbanpolarsweater #witredesign

WOMEN'S URBAN POLAR SWEATER // TORSHOVDALEN, OSLO

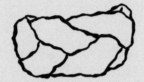

WARM WINTER BRAID

The warm winter braid is a thick, warm headband. It can be worked in three versions on different sized needles, making it different thicknesses. The headband is worked as three strips, knitted in the round to the desired length. These are cast (bound) off, the strips are braided and the ends grafted together with Kitchener stitch.

This pattern is perfect for using up leftover yarn in your stash. The suggested yarns are only a guideline. The version shown is the chunky version.

Sizes:	Narrow(Medium:Chunky)
Approx. width of strip:	Narrow: 3.5cm (1⅜in); Medium: 4.5cm (1¾in); Chunky: 5cm (2in)
Approx. circumference:	Adapt to fit head
Suggested yarns:	Sandnes Alpakka Silke, Dale Pure Eco Wool, Rauma Puno and Rauma Plum
Yarn amount:	Narrow: 2 balls of 50g/200m/218yd Sandnes Alpakka Silke, 4-ply (fingering); Medium: 3 balls of 50g/112m/122yd Dale Pure Eco Wool, DK (8-ply/light worsted) yarn; Chunky: 2 balls of 50g/11m/120yd Rauma Puno, chunky (bulky) yarn and 1 ball of 25g/250m/274yd ball Rauma Plum, 1–3-ply (lace) yarn
Tension:	Narrow: 20 sts to 10cm (4in) square; Medium: 15 sts to 10cm (4in) square; Chunky: 13 sts to 10cm (4in) square – all worked over stocking (stockinette) st on the chosen needle size
Suggested needles:	Narrow: 4mm (UK 8, US 6); Medium: 6mm (UK 4, US 10); Chunky: 8mm (UK 0, US 11) double pointed
Extras:	Four safety pins

Cast on: for narrow version 16 sts on 4mm (UK 8, US 6) needles using 2 strands of Alpakka Silke. For medium version 14 sts on 6mm (UK 4, US 10) using 2 strands of Pure Eco Wool. For chunky version 12 sts on 8mm (UK 0, US 11) needles using 2 strands of Puno and 1 strand of Plum. Work in the round in stocking (stockinette) st until work measures approx. 58cm (22¾in); measure your head and add 2cm (¾in). If you want texture on one side, work as foll: *work 2 rounds in stocking (stockinette) st. On next round: purl for half the round, knit to end of round*. Rep between * and * to end. Remember: you need an extra 2cm (¾in) in length in order to braid the strips together. Rep three times in total.

Place the strips side by side, then secure temporarily with a safety pin at one end so they are attached and do not slip. Braid together. Check that you are braiding evenly. The strips should not bend around the other two strips but flow smoothly. Use three safety pins to attach the ends together firmly at each end of the headband. Sew the ends together using Kitchener st or mattress st. Finally, sew some sts at a few places in the braid so the strips don't slip apart.

Designed together with @strikkolinis

#varmvinterflette #warmwinterbraid #witredesign

Facing page: Grüner beanie with ear flaps on page 14 and children's urban polar sweater on page 46.

Spring

CHILDREN'S URBAN POLAR SWEATER

The urban polar sweater is a soft, warm sweater, knitted using two strands of yarn on big needles. The neckband is made in rib and folded over, making it snug and close-fitting around the neck but not too tight. The zip is practical for putting the sweater on and taking it off but is also an eye-catching detail. The sweater is knitted from the bottom up. Stitches are picked up for the sleeves around the armhole and worked down to the length desired. The zip is sewn in by hand using one strand of Børstet Alpakka.

Sizes:	Age 2(3–4:5–6:7–8:9–10:12:14)
Approx. measurements:	Chest: 67(73:77:83:87:90:93)cm / 26½(28¾:30¼:32¾:34¼:35½:36½)in;
	Length: 39(42:46:49:51:54:57)cm / 15¼(16½:18:19¼:20:21¼:22½)in
Suggested yarns:	Sandnes Peer Gynt and Sandnes Børstet Alpakka
Yarn amount:	3(4:4:5:5:6:6) balls of 50g/91g/98yd Peer Gynt, DK (8-ply/light worsted) yarn; and
	3(3:4:4:5:6:6) balls of 50g/110m/120yd Børstet Alpakka, chunky (bulky) yarn
Tension:	12 sts to 10cm (4in) square over stocking (stockinette) st on 7mm (UK 2, US 10½/11)
Suggested needles:	7mm (UK 2, US 10½/11) circular needle for the front and back; 6mm (UK 4, US 10)
	circular needle for rib and neck
Approx. length of zip:	15(15:15:15:15:20:20)cm / 6(6:6:6:6:7¾:7¾)in. You can adapt the pattern to your
	chosen zip by a couple of centimetres (¾in) or so by making the neck higher or lower.
	It is not recommended to buy a zip that is a lot longer or shorter than the length stated.

Cast on 80(88:92:100:104:108:112) sts on a 6mm (UK 4, US 10) circular needle using 1 strand of each yarn together. Work 5 rounds of k1, p1 rib. Change to a 7mm (UK 2, US, 10½/11) circular needle and stocking (stockinette) st. Place one marker at start of round and one at the halfway point. These mark the sides of the sweater and where you will later divide for the armhole. Work until work measures 24(25:27:29:31:33:35)cm / 9½(9¾:10¾:11½:12¼:13:13¾)in. Cast (bind) off 4 sts at each side, 2 before and 2 after marker.

Front: work back and forth in stocking (stockinette) st across front until work measures 26(30:33:38:40:38:40)cm / 10¼(11¾:13:15:15¾:15:15¾)in. Place marker at centre front, where the zip will be inserted.

Left front: on next RS row, knit until 5 sts before marker. Work these sts in p1, k1 rib and end with k1 (edge st) before marker. Turn and work in patt as set. Rep until work measures 36(38:41:44:46:48:50)cm / 14¼(15:16¼:17¼:18:19:19¾)in. Place the 5 sts at the neck, the rib sts, onto a st holder or waste yarn. Continue to work back and forth in stocking (stockinette) st on the same side. At the same time, on each RS row, knit to last 2 sts before neck edge, k2tog. Rep 3(3:3:4:4:5:5) times in total. Work back and forth across rem sts until work measures 39(42:46:49:51:54:57)cm / 15¼(16½:18:19¼:20:21¼:22½)in. Break yarn. Leave sts on needle or move to a st holder or waste yarn.

Right front: starting at armhole, purl until 5 sts before marker. Work these sts in k1, p1 rib and end with k1 (edge st) before marker. Turn and work in patt as set back the other way. Rep until work measures 36(38:41:44:46:48:50)cm / 14¼(15:16¼:17¼:18:19:19¾)in. Place the 5 sts at the neck, the rib sts, onto a st holder or waste yarn. Continue to work back and forth in stocking (stockinette) st. At the same time, on each WS row, purl to last 2 sts before neck edge, p2tog. Rep 3(3:3:4:4:5:5) times in total. Work back and forth across rem sts until work measures 39(42:46:49:51:54:57)cm / 15¼(16½:18:19¼:20:21¼:22½)in. Break yarn. Leave sts on needle or move to a st holder or waste yarn.

#urbanpolargenser
#urbanpolarsweater
#witredesign

Back: work back and forth until back measures the same length as the fronts. Graft sts on fronts to same number of sts on each side of back. Or cast (bind) off and sew together at shoulders. Leave rem sts for neck on needle.

Neck: knit sts for right front from st holder or waste yarn onto a 6mm (UK 4, US 10) circular needle in rib patt as set. Pick up sts along neck edge. Knit neck sts onto needle in stocking (stockinette) st. Pick up same number of sts along other side of neck. Knit sts on holder for left front onto needle in patt as set. 41(43:43:45:47:49:51) sts. Work back and forth in rib patt as set on front edges and cont rib patt around whole neck so entire neckband is worked in rib. Continue until neckband measures approx. 8(10:10:12:14:18:20)cm / 3¼(4:4:4¾:5½:7:7¾)in. Here you will need to make sure the neckband fits your chosen zip. Remember that the neckband will be folded over double. Cast (bind) off loosely. Check as you cast (bind) off that the edges are stretchy enough.

Zip: fold the neckband over to the inside then sew down by hand using yarn. Start approx. 1cm (½in) in on each side to make room for the zip afterwards. Then insert the zip between the layers of the neck on each side, and down the inside of the opening. It should not go all the way up to the edge. Make sure that the zip is sitting well and is even on both sides. Sew zip in by hand using 1 strand of chunky (bulky) yarn. The sts should be sewn inside the edge st and run all the way to the top and bottom of the zip for the best result.

Sleeves: pick up approx. 12 sts per 10cm (4in) around armhole: approx. 36(36:40:44:48:50:52) sts. Work in the round in stocking (stockinette) st and place a marker at centre underarm on first round. At the same time, k2tog after first st and k2tog before last st at each side of marker every 6 rounds. Work until sleeve measures 24(28:32:34:37:40:43)cm / 9½(11:12½:14½:15¾:17)in or to desired length and dec to 16(16:18:20:20:22:22) sts. Work 5 rounds of k1, p1 rib on 6mm (UK 4, US 10) circular needles. Cast (bind) off in rib. Rep for other sleeve.

Weave in all loose ends.

PERMAFROST SWEATER

The permafrost sweater is worked in two strands of Rauma Pillpi Alpakka chunky (bulky) yarn and one strand of Rauma Lamull (1–3ply/lace weight) yarn. It is a thick and warm sweater with a stylish, slightly cropped design. The sleeves come down over the wrists and are wide before the cuff, which fits closely around the arm. The neckband is semi-high and is doubled over.

When working with this yarn, it can be difficult to see where you have decreased stitches. It is best to use stitch markers as you go.

Sizes:	XS(S:M:L:XL)
Approx. measurements:	Chest: 99(109:118:130:138)cm / 39(43:46½:51:54¼)in;
	Length: 47(50:53:56:59)cm / 18½(19¾:20¾:22:23¼)in
Suggested yarns:	Rauma Pillpi Alpakka and Rauma Lamull
Yarn amount:	10(11:12:13:14) balls of 50g/105m/114yd Rauma Pillpi, bouclé chunky (bulky) yarn;
	and 2(3:3:3:4) balls of 50g/235m/257yd Rauma Lamull, 1–3-ply (lace weight) yarn
Tension:	11 sts to 10cm (4in) square in stocking (stockinette) st
Suggested needles:	7mm (UK 2, US 10½/11) circular needle

Cast on 108(120:130:142:152) sts on a 7mm (UK 2, US 10½/11) circular needle using 1 strand of Lamull and 2 strands of Pillpi together. Place one marker at start of round and one at the halfway point. These mark the armholes. Work 2 rounds of k1, p1 rib to prevent the edge hem from rolling up later. Change to stocking (stockinette) st and work until piece measures 27(29:31:33:35)cm / 10¾(11½:12¼:13:13¾)in. Cast (bind) off 4 sts under each arm, 2 before marker and 2 after it.

Front: work back and forth across front in stocking (stockinette) st until work measures 42(44:47:50:53)cm / 16½(17¼:18½:19¾:20¾)in. On next RS row, cast (bind) off centre 16(16:17:19:20) sts for neck. Cont working back and forth across left front. At the same time, on each WS row, purl to last 2 sts before neck edge, p2tog. Rep twice in total. Work back and forth over rem 15(18:20:22:24) sts until work measures 47(50:53:56:59)cm / 18½(19¾:20¾:22:23¼)in. Place sts on a st holder or waste yarn.

Starting at the right armhole, knit to last 2 sts before neck edge, k2tog. Rep on next RS row so you have dec a total 2 sts at neck. Work back and forth over rem 15(18:20:22:24) sts until work measures 47(50:53:56:59)cm / 18½(19¾:20¾:22:23¼)in. Place sts on a holder or waste yarn.

Back: work back and forth in stocking (stockinette) st until work measures 48(51:54:57:60)cm / 19(20:21¼:22½:23½)in, i.e. 1cm (½in) longer than front. Graft sts on fronts to same number of sts on each side of back. Leave rem sts for neck on needle.

Neck: using the needle on which you have sts for neck, pick up around neck opening. 52(52:54:56:58) sts. Work in the round until neckband measures 11cm (4¼in). Cast (bind) off.

Sleeves: pick up approx. 48(50:50:52:54) sts around armhole and place marker at centre underarm. Cont in stocking (stockinette) st in the round. At the same time, k2tog after first st and k2tog before last st at each side of marker on every third round six times in total. Work until sleeve measures 30(31:32:33:34)cm / 11¾(12¼:12½:13:13½)in or to desired length and dec to 24(26:26:28:30) sts. Work 5 rounds in stocking (stockinette) st. Purl 1 round and work another 5cm (2in) in stocking (stockinette) st. Cast (bind) off. Rep for other sleeve.

Fold in neckband and cuffs and sew down. Weave in all loose ends.

#permafrostsweater
#witredesign

Tips
- *All bodies are different. It is a good idea to measure the knitting against the wearer as you go along.*
- *Remember to check your tension.*
- *Knit the hems down as you cast (bind) off, if desired. It can be difficult to see the stitches using this yarn so it may be easier to cast (bind) off and then sew down. Search for 'cast-off hem for top-down knitting' (or 'knit a folded hem' for similar videos) online.*
- *The sweater is grafted together at the shoulders. Search for videos on 'grafting stocking (stockinette) stitch' or 'Kitchener stitch'.*

CHUNKY BRIOCHE JACKET

The chunky brioche jacket is worked flat using two strands of aran (worsted) yarn on big needles. The back and front are cast on separately to create a split at the sides. This ensures that the stretchy brioche stitch hangs nicely around the waist and hips without bunching up. The front and back are knitted together at the waist and then divided again for the sleeves. The shoulders are cast (bound) off from the wrong side using a third needle (see 'Tips', page 67) for an explanation). This creates a firm but flexible edge that keeps the shoulders in place. All the edging is worked in single strands of yarn on smaller needles. This creates an attractive contrast of textured and smooth knitting.

The jacket is half length with an oversized fit. This pattern therefore uses combined sizing as one size will fit a wide range of people.

Sizes:	XS–S(M:L–XL)
Approx. measurements:	Chest: 111(134:157)cm / 43¾(52¾:61¾)in; Length: 58(61:64)cm / 22¾(24:25¼)in
	measured from the front; Back: approx. 8cm (3¼in) longer
Suggested yarn:	Hip Wool
Yarn amount:	18(20:22) balls of 50g/80m/87yd Hip Wool, aran (10-ply/worsted) yarn
Tension:	7 sts to 10cm (4in) in brioche st on a 10mm (UK 000, US 15) needle;
	16cm to 10cm (4in) in stocking (stockinette) st on a 5mm (UK 6, US 8) needle
Suggested needles:	10mm (UK 000, US 15) and 5mm (UK 6, US 8) circular needles; extra-long (5mm) circular needle
Extras:	Approx. five buttons

Cast on 19(23:27) sts using 2 strands of yarn on a 10mm (UK 000, US 15) circular needle. This will be one side of the front. The sections will be joined later after the split.

Set-up row, RS: *k1, yfwd, s1 loosely purlwise*. Rep from * to *. End with k1 + k1 (edge st). Row 2: k1 (edge st), * yfwd, s1 loosely purlwise. Work next st and yfwd together*. Rep from * to *. End with yfwd, s1 loosely purlwise + k1 (edge st). Row 3: k1 (edge st). *Knit next st and yfwd together, yfwd, s1 loosely purlwise*. Rep from * to *. End by knitting next st and yfwd together + k1 (edge st).

Rep rows 2 and 3 until work measures 21cm (8¼in) ending with a WS row. Set work aside on an extra needle or waste yarn, and work another front in the same way described above.

After working both fronts as above, you are ready to start the back. Cast on 39(47:55) sts using 2 strands of yarn on a 10mm (UK 000, US 15) circular needle and rep the rows as shown for front until work measures 29cm (11½in) ending with a WS row.

Starting with one front, work 1 row from RS but stop when 1 st rem on needle. Pick up the back and knit the last st on the front and the first st on the back together. Work rest of back but stop when 1 st rem on needle. Knit last st on back and first st on next front together. The sts that have been knitted together now mark the sides of the jacket. Add a marker or mark with waste yarn here.

Work in patt as set until jacket measures 33(35:37)cm / 13(13¾:14½)in measured from the front. On next RS row, create a new st in marked sts by knitting into the front and the back of the st. The two sts worked in the marked sts are the new edge sts on each side of the armhole. Rep on both sides and work to end of row. Leave the work on the needle and use new needles to work fronts separately.

Left side of front: work back and forth in patt as set. On next RS row, work to last 2 sts at neck, k2tog. Rep on every third RS row, i.e. on every sixth row, 4(4:6) times in total. You now have 15(19:21) sts on your needles. Cont until work measures 53(56:59)cm / 20¾(22:23¼)in measured from the front. Leave sts on needle.

Right side of front: start at armhole and rep almost as described for left front. The difference is that the sts at the neck are purled together on WS. Leave sts on needle.

Back: work over the 39(47:55) sts for back until work is the same length as the fronts measured from the armholes. On next RS row, work 15(19:21) sts, cast (bind) off 9(9:13) sts and work rem 15(19:21) sts.

Cast (bind) off and seam together with a third needle as described under 'Tips'; or you can graft together with Kitchener st or cast (bind) off and sew together using a sewing needle and mattress st.

Continued overleaf.

#chunkypatentjakke
#chunkybriochejacket
#witredesign

Sleeves: start at underarm and pick up 29(33:37) sts around armhole. Round 1 is worked from the RS by knitting into the back leg of the st to prevent holes. Rep the set-up row + rows 2 and 3 at the start of the instructions. Rounds 1 and 2 are thus worked in the round before working the sleeve back and forth. Work until sleeve measures approx. 30cm (11¾in) or to desired length. Break off 1 strand of yarn and change to a 5mm (UK 6, US 8) circular needle. Work 5cm (2in) in stocking (stockinette) st in the round and then purl 1 round. Work another 4.5cm (1½in) in stocking (stockinette) st. Knit down and cast (bind) off. Sew sleeve together. Rep for other sleeve. Remember to knit the other edging bands in the right order.

Bottom band: pick up approx. 59(71:83) sts divided evenly around bottom of back using a single strand of yarn on a 5mm (UK 6, US 8) circular needle. Work 5cm (2in) in stocking (stockinette) st and one purl row. Work another 4.5cm (1½in) in stocking (stockinette) st. Knit edge down and cast (bind) off. Pick up approx. 30(36:42) sts at the bottom of each front and rep as described above.

Sides of split: pick up approx. 40 sts evenly along side edge of front using single strand yarn on a 5mm (UK 6, US 8) circular needle. Work 3cm (1¼in) in stocking (stockinette) st then one purl row. Work another 2.5cm (1in) in stocking (stockinette) st. Knit edge down and cast (bind) off. Pick up approx. 50 sts evenly along side edge of back and rep as described above. Rep for the split on the other side. Sew the sections together at the top of the split. Place the edge for the back on top.

Front bands and neckband: for best results, work entire band in one using an extra-long circular needle, or by joining the cables together. Otherwise, the different bands can be worked separately and sewn together at the end. If doing this, avoid joins in highly visible places. It is important to pick up sts evenly around the edges so be sure to use a tape measure.

Pick up 16 sts per 10cm (4in) from the bottom edge of bottom band on right side and round to the bottom edge of bottom band on left side. This is equivalent to approx. 226(236:246) sts in total. On first WS row, work all sts into the back leg of the st to prevent holes and dec down to the correct number of sts if you have too many. Work in stocking (stockinette) st for approx. 2.5cm (1in). Place work on a table and place markers where you want buttonholes. It is important to get a result that you are happy with. Continue in stocking (stockinette) st and cast (bind) off 2 sts at each marker. On next row, cast on 2 new sts at each marker. Work until band measures 5cm (2in) in total and work one purl row. Work another 4.5cm (1¾in) and work buttonholes again so that they will be in the same place on this side when the band is folded over to the inside. Knit edge down and cast (bind) off. Sew around the buttonholes with yarn to produce an even, sturdy edge.

Weave in all ends and sew on buttons. Press the stocking (stockinette) st bands if necessary.

AMÉLIE SWEATER

The Amélie sweater is knitted in one strand of 1–3-ply (lace weight) yarn and one strand of 5-ply (sport) yarn. It is a delicate and slightly oversized sweater, knitted in the round and then cut up the sides at the end. You can choose to knit the whole sweater back and forth, one piece at a time, by not adding the extra steek stitches between front and back. The sweater is basically a simple sweater but with extra length at the back and a stylish high split running all the way up to the armhole on both sides. The sweater is held together with an attractive band knitted between the front and back at the end. This means that the Amélie sweater will hang well on the body, making the split a great detail on an otherwise simple everyday garment.

Sizes:	XS(S:M:L:XL)
Approx. measurements:	Chest: 102(112:121:129:137)cm / 40¼(44:47¾:50¾:54)in;
	Length: 47(50.53.56.59)cm / 18½(19¾:20¾:22:23¼)in
Suggested yarns:	Rauma Finull and Rauma Plum
Yarn amount:	5(6:7:8:8) balls of 50g/175m/191yd Rauma Finull, 5-ply (sport) yarn;
	4(5:5:6:6) balls of 25g/250m/273yd Rauma Plum, 1–3-ply (lace weight) yarn
Tension:	19 sts to 10cm (4in) square over stocking (stockinette) st using 4mm (UK 8, US 6) needles
Suggested needles:	4mm (UK 8, US 6) circular needle and 3.5 (UK 10/9, US 4) circular needle for rib

---

Front rib: cast on 97(107:115:123:131) sts on a 3.5mm (UK 10/9, US 4) circular needle using 1 strand of each yarn together. Work back and forth in rib as foll: k1 (edge st), k1, p1 to end of row, ending with p1, k1, k1 (edge st). On WS row, slip first st loosely for a neat edge. Work in rib in patt as set until work measures 5cm (2in). Set work aside.

Back rib: cast on for rib and work 5cm (2in) in rib as for front. On next RS row, change to 4mm (UK 8, US 6) needle and to stocking (stockinette) st but cont in patt as set for first 3 and last 3 sts in row. Cont working back and forth until whole work measures 15cm (6in) ending with a RS row.

Now you are going to knit both front and back onto the same circular needle and cast on extra steek sts between front and back, which will be cut at the end.

Cont with back on 4mm (UK 8, US 6) needle and cast on 15 new sts at end of row. Add a marker here to mark start of round. Knit sts from front onto needle in stocking (stockinette) st, here too keeping rib patt as set for first 3 and 3 last sts. Cast on 15 new sts once front is on the needle. You now have 224(244:260:276:292) sts in total. The new sts between front and back are worked in stocking (stockinette) st, apart from the centre st, which is always purled (this marks the st that will be cut at the end). Work in the round in patt as set until front measures 27(29:31:33:35)cm / 10¾(11½:12¼:13:13¾)in.

To mark armhole: cast (bind) off the 15 new sts on each side + 4 extra sts before and after them, making a total of 23 sts cast (bind) off on each side. Cont in the round and cast on 9 new sts between front and back. You now have 196(216:232:248:264) sts on your needle. Cont in stocking (stockinette) st in the round apart from centre steek sts, which are always purled here too.

When front measures 39(41:43:45:47)cm / 15¼(16¼:17:17¾:18½)in, cast (bind) off centre 13(13:15:17:19) sts on front. Cont working back and forth over all sts in patt as set. At the same time, k2tog or p2tog at end of each row until you have dec a total 6(8:8:10:10) sts on each side. Cont working back and forth until front measures 47(50:53:56:59)cm / 18½(19¾:20¾:22:23¼)in.

On next RS row, knit sts for left front onto a st holder. Cast (bind) off the first 5 steek sts that were cast on between this front and back = 4 sts in stocking (stockinette) st + purl st. Work across the next 4 steek sts, the back and the next 4 steek sts. Cast (bind) off 5 steek sts = purl st + 4 sts in stocking (stockinette) st that were cast on at the other side. Then knit sts for right side of front onto a st holder. Break yarn.

Continued overleaf.

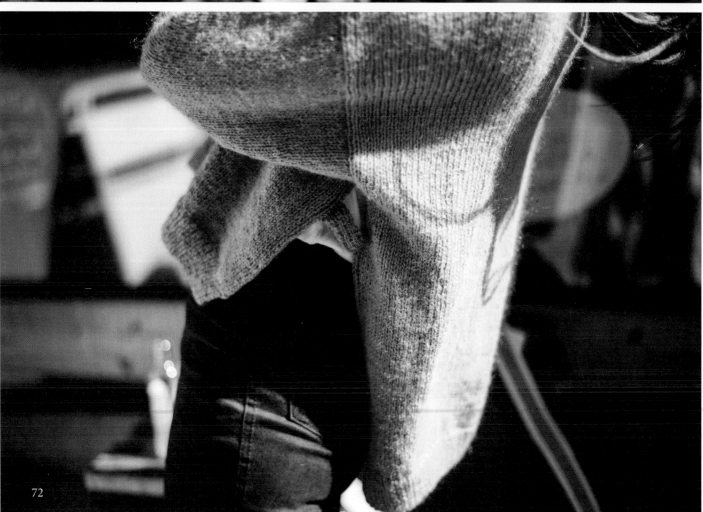

Back: work sts for back + the 4 steek sts on each side in stocking (stockinette) st until back measures 1cm (½in) longer than the fronts. On last row, cast (bind) off the 4 steek sts on each side. Graft sts on fronts to same number of sts on each side of back. Place neck sts onto a 3.5mm (UK 9/10, US 4) needle.

Neck: pick up sts round neck edge using the 3.5mm (UK 9/10, US 4) needle used for the neck. You should have approx. 82(86:90:94:98) sts in total incl back neck sts. Work in the round in k1, p1 rib until neckband measures 3cm (1¼in). Cast (bind) off in rib.

Making up: before you can work the sleeves, you need to cut the sweater at the sides: then sew using a zigzag st along each side of the purled centre st of each steek added at sides using one strand of 1–3-ply (lace weight) yarn. Do this on both sides of the body and both sides of the armhole. Cut the purl centre st so the work splits in two. Fold steek edges in and press down to create a firm folded edge. Fold the edge in once more, hiding the cut edge inside the fold. The steeks at the armhole are not as wide because you will need to pick up sts here for the sleeve afterwards. The steeks for the body have more sts to work with because this edge will be visible when the sweater is worn. Sew down by hand with 1 strand of Plum.

Sleeves: start under armhole and pick up sts evenly around the edge until you reach under the armhole on the other side. You should have approx. 78(82:86:90:94) sts in total. Dec down to correct number of sts on first round if necessary. Hold back and front together and work sleeve in the round. Knit last st on needle together with first st on needle, and place a marker around this st, which will be at the centre underarm. Cont in stocking (stockinette) st in the round, knitting the 2 sts after and the 2 sts before the marker together every 2cm (¾in) 18(18:20:20:22) times in total. Work until sleeve measures 36(38:40:42:44)cm / 14¼(15:15¾:16½:17¼)in or to desired length. Dec to 40(40:42:42:44) sts. Change to 3.5mm (UK 9/10, US 4) needle and work k1, p1 rib until cuff measures 5cm (2in). Cast (bind) off in rib. Rep for other sleeve.

Bands: pick up 7 sts along edge of split, approx. 8cm (3¼in) below armhole. k1 (edge st), k1, p1 and end with k1 (edge st). Work back and forth in patt as set until band measures 7cm (2¾in). Cast (bind) off and sew band down to edge on other side of split. Rep on other side of sweater.

Weave in all loose ends.

#améliesweater #witredesign

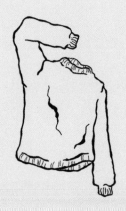

COLLETT SWEATER

The Collett sweater is a sweater with attractive shoulder detailing and a narrow, semi-high neck. The armholes are quite deep and the body wide. It is knitted in one strand of 5-ply (sport weight) yarn and two strands of 1–3-ply (lace weight) yarn. The sleeves are therefore narrow at the bottom for a slimmer fit.

The sweater is knitted from the top down. First, stitches are increased for the body to produce the attractive shoulder detail, before going on to increase for both the body and the sleeves at the same time. The sweater is finished off with short rows at the bottom to make it a little longer at the back than the front before the rib hem. There is no making up involved and the pattern is easy to adapt as it can be tried on as you go.

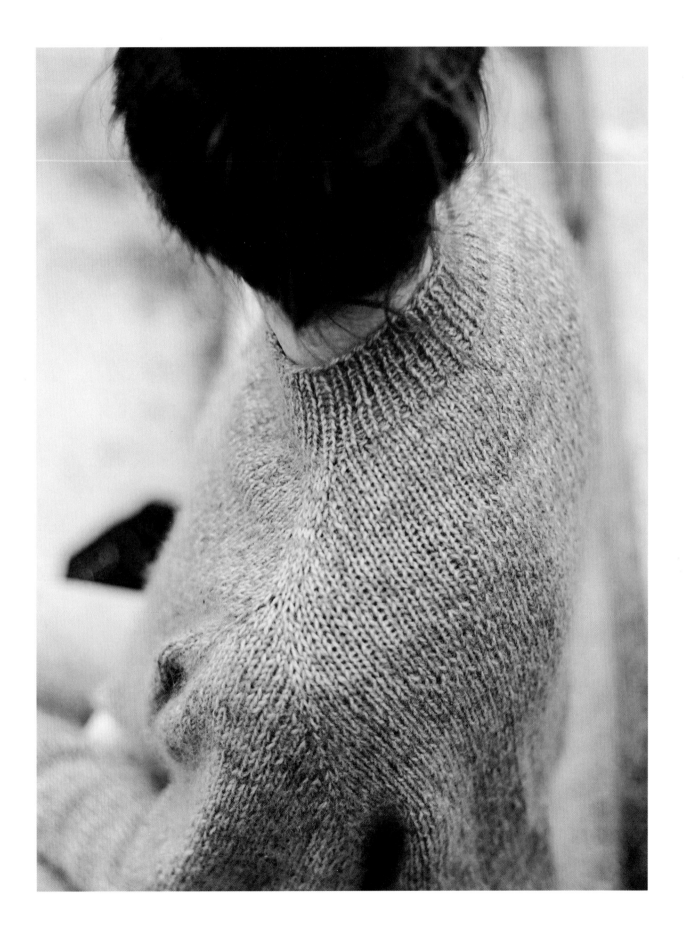

Sizes:	XS(S:M:L:XL)
Approx. measurements:	Chest: 96(104:111:119:126)cm / 37¾(41:43¾:46¾:49½)in;
	Length at centre front: 52(55:58:61:64)cm / 20½(21¼:22¾:24:25¼)in
Suggested yarns:	Rauma Finull and Rauma Plum
Yarn amount:	5(5:5:6:6) balls of 50g/175m/191yd Rauma Finull, 5-ply (sport) yarn;
	7(7:8:9:9) balls of 25g/250m/273yd Rauma Plum, 1–3-ply (lace weight) yarn
Tension:	16 sts to 10cm (4in) in stocking (stockinette) st on 4.5mm (UK 7, US 7) needle;
	20 sts to 10cm (4in) in rib on 3.5mm (UK 9/10, US 4) needle
Suggested needles:	3.5mm (UK 9/10, US 4) and 4.5mm (UK 7, US 7) circular needles

---

Cast on 72(80:88:96:104) sts on a 3.5mm (UK 9/10, US 4) circular needle using 1 strand of Finull and 2 strands of Plum. Work 5cm (2in) in k1, p1 rib. On last round of rib, place markers around foll sts: 1, 35, 37, 71 (1, 39, 41, 79 : 1, 43, 45, 87 : 1, 47, 49, 95 : 1, 51, 53, 103). Also place a marker at centre front, which will be the starting point for short rows when shaping the neck.

Change to a 4.5mm (UK 7, US 7) circular needle. Work raglan on each RS round at the same time as working short rows as described below:

Raglan (body only): inc for raglan on the outside of the 2 marked sts on each side. This means that the shoulder detail is created over 3 sts. The raglan increases are worked on every alt round by picking up the strand of yarn on the outside of the marked st and knitting into it. While you are working the short rows, at the same time, work the raglan increases on every RS row. At right side of marked st, m1 to right, at left side of marked st, m1 to left. Inc five times in total = 92(100:108:116:124) sts.

Short rows for neck: work until 14 sts rem before centre front marker, turn and purl back the other way until 14 sts rem before centre front marker. Cont as set, turning 2 sts nearer to marker each time. Turn five times each side in total. Cont in stocking (stockinette) st in the round. Now you will be increasing for both body and sleeves at the same time:

Raglan (body and sleeves): on inside of marked sts, inc for sleeves every alt round as foll: work marked st. Pick up yarn to make a new st and m1 to the left. Work up to st before next marked st, pick up yarn to make a new st and twist to the right. The new sts will thus be turned away from the marked sts. On outside of marked sts, continue to inc as before. After 3 increases for sleeves and a total 8 increases for body, including previous increases, cont increasing on every fourth round for body = 116(124:132:140:148) sts.

Cont as described above, on every alt round for sleeves and every fourth round for body until you have increased for sleeves 24(26:28:30:32) times in total = 51(55:59:63:67) sts for each sleeve including marked sts. Cont working across all sts, now increasing for body on every round until you have increased for body 20(21:22:23:24) times in total (including increases at top shoulder) = 248(268:288:308:328) sts.

Continued overleaf.

On next round, place sts for sleeves, including marked raglan sts onto a st holder or waste yarn = 51(55:59:63:67) sts for each sleeve. Cast on 4 new sts at each side and place a marker in centre. Cont working stocking (stockinette) st in the round over all body sts, 154(166:178:190:202) sts in total, until work measures 47(50:53:56:59)cm / 18½(19¾:20¾:22:23¼)in measured from under neckband at centre front. Then work short rows at back as explained below:

Short rows for back, at bottom of body: work back in stocking (stockinette) st until 5 sts before side marker. Turn and work until 5 sts before marker at other side. Turn and work until 15 sts before marker. Cont as set, 10 sts longer each time, until you have turned four times on each side in total. Then work to centre back. Change to 3.5mm (UK 9/10, US 4) needle and work k1, p1 rib around whole body for 5cm (2in). Cast (bind) off in rib.

Sleeves: place sts for sleeve on a 4.5mm (UK 7, US 7) circular needle and pick up 4 new sts in the new sts you added at the underarm. 55(59:63:67:71) sts. Place a marker at centre underarm. Work in stocking (stockinette) st in the round, at the same time decreasing on either side of marker as foll: after marker, k2tog. Before marker, k2tbl. Rep every 3.5cm (1⅜in), eight times in total until 39(43:47:51:55) sts rem on needle. Work until sleeve measures 39(40:41:42:42) cm / 15¼(15¾:16¼:16½:16½)in or to desired length. Change to 3.5mm (UK 9/10, US 4) needle and dec 11 sts on round 1, while working k1, p1 rib. Work in rib until cuff measures 5cm (2in). Cast (bind) off in rib. Rep for other sleeve.

Weave in all loose ends. Press/block the raglan increases well, and the top of front and back, so the sweater hangs well when worn.

#collettsweater #witredesign

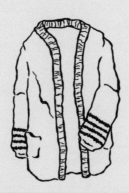

FUZZY SIBERIAN JACKET

The fuzzy Siberian jacket is a soft, light jacket with striped sleeves. It is knitted from the bottom up, divides for the front and back and is grafted back together at the shoulders. Stitches are picked up around the armholes for the sleeves. The sleeves are knitted down over the wrist, ending with an attractive i-cord edge. The fuzzy Siberian jacket is slightly oversized and has deep pockets. Because the yarn used in this jacket is so light, it doesn't have buttons, to prevent it from sagging.

Sizes:	XS(S:M:L:XL)
Approx. measurements:	Chest: 105(115:125:135:145)cm / 41½(45¼:49¼:53:57)in; Length: 63(66:69:72:75)cm / 24¾(26:27¼:28¼:29½)in
Suggested yarn:	Rauma Iris
Yarn amount:	7(8:9:10:11) balls of 50g/130m/142yd Rauma Iris, chunky (bulky) yarn; 1 ball each of same yarn in two contrasting shades
Tension:	10 sts to 10cm (4in) square over stocking (stockinette) st using 8mm (UK 0, US 11) needles
Suggested needles:	7mm (UK 2, US 10½/11) and 8mm (UK 0, US 11) circular needles

Cast on 94(104:114:124:134) sts on a 7mm (UK 2, US 10½/11) circular needle using 2 strands of yarn and work rib patt as set: k1 (edge st), k1, p1 to end of row and end with k1 (edge st). Work in rib as set for 4cm (1½in). Change to an 8mm (UK 0, US 11) circular needle. Cont in stocking (stockinette) st, at the same time increasing 11 sts evenly around round 1. Place a marker after 26(28:31:33:36) sts and 26(28:31:33:36) sts before end of round. These mark the sides. Work until work measures 22(24:26:28:30)cm / 8¾(9½:10¼11:11¾)in.

Pockets: on next RS row, work 13 sts and cast (bind) off next 15 sts. Set work aside. *Cast on 15 sts on a spare 8mm (UK 0, US 11) circular needle and work in stocking (stockinette) st until pocket measures 14cm (5½in) or desired length*. Knit pocket into body where you have just cast (bind) off sts. Continue until 28 sts rem and cast (bind) off 15 sts. Set work aside. Make another pocket, as at * – * above, and knit onto needle. Cont in stocking (stockinette) st over all sts until work measures 43(45:47:49:51)cm / 17(17¾:18½:19¾:20)in.

Right front: on next RS row, *knit edge st, k2tog*. Work to side marker, turn and purl back the other way. Rep from * to * on each RS row, 8(9:10:11:12) times in total. Cont in stocking (stockinette) st until armhole measures 20(21:22:23:24)cm / 7¾(8¼:8¾:9:9½)in. Place sts on a st holder or waste yarn.

Back: work back and forth in stocking (stockinette) st until back measures 1cm (½in) longer than front. Graft sts on back and front together for the best result. Or cast (bind) off and sew together at shoulders with grafting st. Leave rem sts for neck on needle.

Left front: starting at armhole, *knit to last 3 sts. k2tog tbl, k1 (edge st)*. Rep from * to * on each RS row, 8(9:10:11:12) times in total. Cont in stocking (stockinette) st until armhole measures 20(21:22:23:24)cm / 7¾(8¼:8¾:9:9½)in. Graft sts on back and front together at shoulder, as described above.

Continued overleaf.

Tips
• *All bodies are different. It is a good idea to measure the knitting against the wearer as you go along.*
• *Remember to check your tension.*

Front bands in rib: for best results, this ribbed edge should be worked in one on a long circular needle. Or it can be knitted, e.g. in two parts and joined together at the end.

Start at bottom of right side and pick up approx. 14 sts per 10cm (4in) on a 7mm (UK 2, US 10½/11) circular needle. Use a tape measure and pick up sts evenly. Knit sts for neck onto needle and pick up same number of sts down left side. Turn and work k1, p1 rib + p1 as last st. Inc or dec as necessary to make sure there is an odd number of sts on row 1.

Work rib in pattern as set for 4cm (1½in) and cast (bind) off loosely in rib.

Sleeves: pick up approx. 44(46:48:50:52) sts around armhole. Place marker at start of round. Work in stocking (stockinette) st in the round, and k2tog before and after the marker every 5cm (2in). Work until sleeve measures 22cm (8¾in).

Stripes in contrasting yarn: (remember to continue the decreases). Work 2 rounds dark and 4 rounds white (or your own preferred shades). Rep three times in total ending with 2 rounds in the dark shade.

Cont in main colour until sleeve measures approx. 38cm (15in). Measure on the wearer – the sleeves should be slightly short. Dec evenly to 22(24:24:26:26) sts. Change to a 7mm (UK 2, US 10½/11) circular needle and cast on 4 new sts.

Work an i-cord cast-(bind-)off as foll:

Turn work so you are working from WS. K3, slip next 2 sts loosely, one by one, knitwise and then slip them back to left-hand needle. K2tog tbl. Slip sts on right-hand needle back onto left-hand needle. Rep until 2 sts rem on needle. K2tog. Rep for other sleeve.

Weave in all loose ends and sew pockets down on inside.

#fuzzysibirjakke #fuzzysiberianjacket #witredesign

CROPPED WESTERN TEE

The cropped western tee is a loose and airy T-shirt. The narrow sleeves make for a good fit while the wide neck gives it a stylish shape. The T-shirt is knitted from the bottom up with short rows, making it longer at the back. It has an attractive raglan sleeve and new short rows at the neck to make the neckline lower at the front. Knit the body to your desired length before working the sleeves.

Sizes:	XS(S:M:L:XL)
Approx. measurements:	Chest: 90(98:106:114:120)cm / 35½(38½:41¾:44¾:47¼)in; Length: 41(44:47:50:53)cm / 16¼(17¼:18½:19¾:20¾)in measured from front
Suggested yarn:	Rauma Petunia
Yarn amount:	4(5:6:7:7) balls of 50g/110m/120yd Rauma Petunia, DK (8-ply, light worsted) yarn
Tension:	20 sts to 10cm (4in) square over stocking (stockinette) st using 4mm (UK 8, US 6 needles)
Suggested needles:	3.5mm (UK 9/10, US 4) and 4mm (UK 8, US 6) circular needles

Cast on 180(196:212:228:240) sts using a 3.5mm (UK 9/10, US 4) circular needle. Place one marker at start of round and one at the halfway point. These mark the sides. Place another marker at centre front. Work k1, p1 rib until neckband measures 1cm (½in).

Now work short rows on first round after rib as foll: change to a 4mm (UK 8, US 6) circular needle and knit until 31 sts before the marker that indicates the start of round. Turn and work until 30 sts before marker at other side. Rep turns, knitting 10 sts further towards marker each time (you will eventually be knitting the front). Turn seven times each side in total.

Cont in stocking (stockinette) st in the round until work measures 20(22:24:26:28)cm / 7¾(8¾:9½:10¼:11)in measured from the front. Cast (bind) off 4 sts at each side, 2 before and 2 after marker. Set work aside.

Sleeves: cast on 56(60:64:68:72) sts on a 3.5mm (UK 9/10, US 4) circular needle. Work in the round in k1, p1 rib until rib measures 1cm (½in). Change to a 4mm (UK 8, US 6) circular needle and work in stocking (stockinette) st in the round until sleeve measures 8cm (3¼in) in total. Cast (bind) off 4 sts at centre underarm. Knit sleeve into circular needle for body.

Make other sleeve in the same way and knit it into the other side of the body.

Raglan: on round 1, once all the sections are on the same needle, knit first and last st at each of the joins together and place a marker in this st. This marker marks where you will work raglan decreases as foll:

Next round, work until 1 st before next marker. Sl2 loosely as if knitting together. K1 and lift the 2 sts on right-hand needle over this st. This st will continue to mark the raglan. Rep for all markers in round (8 sts dec in total) and work 1 round without decreases. Dec in this way on every alt round eight times in total. Then dec on each round until 24(26:28:30:32) sts rem for each sleeve. Don't count the marker st.

Now work short rows for neck while continuing to dec as described above, on every alt row, i.e. every RS row.

Turn and work until 10 sts before centre front marker. Turn and work until 10 sts before centre front marker on other side. Rep turns, turning 2 sts earlier each time. Rep a total 6(7:8:9:10) turns on each side (12 sts rem for each sleeve). On the next row it is important to turn neatly for a neat final result. Watch videos as mentioned in 'Tips' and check how to use the method you have chosen.

Change to a 3.5mm (UK 9/10, US 4) circular needle and work k1, p1 rib. The marked sts must always be knit sts so that the raglan ends neatly. Therefore k2tog in each section to make sure that the k1, p1 rib works out (4 sts decreased). Work in rib until neckband measures 1cm (½in). Cast (bind) off in rib. Make sure that the neck isn't too loose.

Weave in all loose ends and sew up the hole at the underarm. Add a couple of sts around the neck if there are holes.

#croppedwesterntee #witredesign

Tips
• *All bodies are different. It is a good idea to measure the knitting against the wearer as you go along.*
• *Remember to check your tension.*
• *Search for videos on 'short rows' online to see the technique in more detail.*
• *The length is measured from the top of the shoulder at the neck and down the length of the front, including the rib.*

Summer

KIDS' NORDIC SUMMER TOP

The kids' Nordic summer top is a simple top with airy
stitches, perfect for hot days. It is knitted from the bottom
up using two strands of DK (light worsted) yarn on big
needles. The top is snug, yet cool, and is knitted in thick
yarn, which also means it hangs well.

Sizes:	Age 1(2:4:6:8:10:12)
Approx. measurements:	Chest: 50(53:57:63:67:70:73)cm / 19¾(20¾:22½:24¾: 26½:27½:28¾)in;
	Length: 28(30:33:36:40:44:47)cm / 11(11¼:13:14¼:15¾: 17¼:18½)in
Suggested yarn:	Rauma Pelini
Yarn amount:	2(2:2:3:3:3:4) balls of 50g/102m/111yd Rauma Pelini, DK (8-ply/light worsted) yarn
Tension:	12 sts to 10cm (4in) square over stocking (stockinette) st
Suggested needles:	8mm (UK 0, US 11) circular needle

Cast on 60(64:68:76:80:84:88) sts using 2 strands of yarn on an 8mm (UK 0, US 11) circular needle. Place one marker at start of round and one halfway round. These mark armholes. Work stocking (stockinette) st in the round until work measures 17(19:21:23:25:27:29)cm / 6¾(7½:8¼:9:9¾:10¾:11½)in.

Place another marker at centre front. Divide for front and back by repeating foll dec rounds: work to last 2 sts before marker at armhole and k2tog. Turn, sl1 with yarn in front and purl back the other way. Work to last 2 sts before other armhole marker and p2tog. Slip first st of next row loosely with yarn in front here too. Rep 3(4:4:4:5:5:5) times each side in total.

On next RS row, work to marker at centre front and cast (bind) off 2(2:3:3:3:4:4) sts neatly. Cont towards armhole *to last 2 sts, k2tog at end of row as before. Turn, purl back until last 2 sts before neck, k2tog*. Rep from * to * once more. Continue knitting last 2 sts before neck together on every WS row, but only dec every other time at armhole, i.e. on every fourth row. Rep until you have 3 sts on your needle. Work across these sts until work measures approx. 28(30:33:36:40:44:47) cm / 11(11¾:13:14¼:15¾:17¼:18½)in or desired length. The length of the straps should fit the wearer. Leave sts on a safety pin.

Start at centre front from WS and cast (bind) off 2(2:3:3:3:4:4) sts neatly.

Rep as described above.

Make back the same way as front. For the neatest result, graft straps for back to straps for front, or cast (bind) off and sew together at shoulders. Weave in all loose ends and press bottom edge to prevent it rolling up.

#nordisksommertoppbarn #nordicsummertopkids #witredesign

Tips
- *All bodies are different. It is a good idea to measure the knitting against the wearer as you go along.*
- *Remember to check your tension.*
- *The stitches at the neck and armhole will not be picked up for a neckband or sleeve. This means that it is important to work edge stitches as knit stitches for an attractive result. Always slip first st off loosely. If the previous row was a knit row, the yarn must be at the front. If the previous row was a purl row, the yarn must be at the back.*

KIDS' NORDIC SUMMER DRESS

The kids' Nordic summer dress is a simple, basic A-line dress. It is knitted from the bottom up using two strands of cotton yarn on big needles and has airy stitches, perfect for hot days. The dress might feel heavy when on the needles but it hangs attractively and fits the wearer snugly.

Sizes:	Age 1(2:4:6:8:10:12)
Approx. measurements:	Circumference around bottom edge: 56(62:68:74:80:84:92)cm / 22(24½:26¾:29¼:31½:33:36¼)in;
	Chest at underarm: 49(52:55:63:65:71:74)cm / 19¼(20½:21¾:24¾:25½:28:29¼)in;
	Length including strap: 42(45:52:60:68:76:80)cm / 16½(17¾:20½:23½:26¾:30:31½)in
Suggested yarn:	Rauma Pelini
Yarn amount:	3(3:5:6:7:8:9) balls of 50g/102m/111yd Rauma Pelini, DK (8-ply/light worsted) yarn
Tension:	13 sts to 10cm (4in) square over stocking (stockinette) st
Suggested needles:	7mm (UK 2, US 10½/11) circular needle

Cast on 72(80:88:96:104:112:120) sts using 2 strands of yarn on a 7mm (UK 2, US 10½/11) circular needle. Place one marker at start of round and one halfway round. These mark sides of dress. Work in stocking (stockinette) st until work measures 16(16:18:20:22:24:26)cm / 6¼(6¼:7:7¾:8¾: 9½:10¼)in. Now dec down sides evenly. *Work 1 st after marker, k2tog. Work to 3 sts before next marker, k2tog tbl, k1*. Rep between * and * at both markers every 4(4:5:6:6:6:6) cm / 1½(1½:2:2½:2½:2½:2½)in 2(3:4:4:5:5:6) times in total. 64(68:72:80:84:92:96) sts rem on needle. Work in stocking (stockinette) st until work measures 30(33:39:46:53:59:62)cm / 11¾(13:15¼:18:20¾:23¼:24½)in. Cast (bind) off 1 st before marker and 1 st after marker at both sides.

Place a new marker at centre front and rep foll dec rows to shape armholes and neck: work to last 2 sts before marker at armhole, k2tog. Turn, sl1 with yarn in front and purl back the other way. Work to last 2 sts before other armhole marker, k2tog. Slip first st loosely with yarn in front here too. Rep 2(3:3:3:4:4:5) times each side in total.

On next RS row, work to marker at centre front and cast (bind) off 2(3:3:3:4:4:4) sts neatly. Cont towards armhole and *k2tog at the end of the row as before. Turn, purl back until last 2 sts before neck, k2tog*. Rep from * to * once more. Continue decreasing 2 sts at neck edge as set on every alt row, but only dec every alt time at armhole, i.e. on every fourth row. Rep until you have 3 sts on your needle. Work across these sts until work measures approx. 40(45:52:60:68:76:80)cm / 15¾(17¾:20½:23½:26¾:30:31½)in or to desired length. Leave sts on a safety pin.

Start at centre front from WS and cast (bind) off 2(3:3:3:4:4:5) sts.

Work other side of front as described above but reverse shaping.

Make back of dress the same way as front. For the neatest result graft straps together, or cast (bind) off and sew together at shoulders.

Weave in all loose ends and press bottom edge to prevent it rolling up.

#nordisksommerkjolebarn #nordicsummerdresskids #witredesign

Tips
• All bodies are different. It is a good idea to measure the knitting against the wearer as you go along.
• Remember to check your tension.
• The stitches at the neck and armhole will not be picked up for a neckband or sleeve. This means that it is important to work edge stitches as knit stitches for an attractive result. Always slip first st off loosely. If the previous row was a knit row, the yarn must be at the front. If the previous row was a purl row, the yarn must be at the back.
• The front and back of the dress look the same.

BASIC TUBE TOP

Sometimes all you need is a very simple basic garment, so why not knit it yourself? Here is a very simple tube top that works well for everyday wear and special occasions. Wide elastic at the top means that the top fits well and the light, airy stitches make it great for hot summer days. The basic tube top is knitted from the top down so the length can be easily adjusted – it can be made shorter to wear with high-waisted trousers and skirts, or a bit longer to skim the waist. Or, if you feel able, you could make it long enough to be worn as a tube dress.

| Sizes: | XS(S:M:L:XL) |

Approx. measurements: Chest: 65(75:85:95:105)cm / 25½(29½:33½:37½:41½)in;
Length: 32(34:37:40:43)cm / 12½(13½:14½:15¾:17)in

Suggested yarn: Rauma Petunia

Yarn amount: 3(4:5:6:7) balls of 50g/110m/120yd Rauma Petunia,
DK (8-ply/light worsted)

Tension: 13 sts to 10cm (4in) square over stocking (stockinette) st

Suggested needles: 7mm (UK 2, US 10½/11) circular needle

Extras: 3cm (1¼in) wide elastic for casing at upper edge – the length should measure
the circumference of your trunk, just below your armpits, minus 5cm (2in).
The elastic should be a similar colour to the chosen yarn.

Cast on 84(97:110:123:136) sts using 2 strands of yarn on a 7mm (UK 2, US 10½/11) circular needle and place a marker at start of round. Knit 6 rounds. Purl 1 round – this will form the folded edge at the top. Knit 6 rounds. Fold the cast-on row over to the inside and knit down now to form a casing, if you wish. Remember to leave 3–4 sts open by the marker so you can thread the elastic in at the end. Alternatively, you can sew the casing down once the whole top is finished.

Work in stocking (stockinette) st until top measures 32(34:37:40:43)cm / 12½(13½:14½:15¾:17)in from folded edge or to desired length. Cast (bind) off.

If you wish, you could add a different finish for the bottom hem; for example, rib, moss st or an i-cord cast off. Insert wide elastic in the casing at upper edge so the top fits you snugly.

Weave in all loose ends.

#heltenkeltubetopp #basictubetop #witredesign

> **Tips**
> • *All bodies are different. It is a good idea to measure the knitting against the wearer as you go along.*
> • *Remember to check your tension.*
> • *A casing for elastic is worked at the upper edge. The edge can be knitted down as you go. If you want to try it out, search for videos on how to 'knit a casing'.*

MIDSUMMER CULOTTES

The Midsummer culottes are a wide trouser with short, straight legs. The culottes have a high waist with wide elastic to ensure a good fit. They are knitted using two strands of DK (light worsted) yarn on big needles. The knitting may feel heavy on the needles and take a lot of yarn, but they will hang well when worn and are airy for summer wear.

Shown with the basic tube top on page 104.

Tips
• All bodies are different. It is a good idea to measure the knitting against the wearer as you go along.
• Remember to check your tension.
• The culottes can be knitted to the desired length. The amount of yarn in the instructions is for the measurements stated.
– A casing for elastic is created at the waist. The edge can be knitted down as you go. If you want to try it out, search for 'knit a casing' online to see a video.
• The elastic should be stretched enough that the yarn gathers slightly at the waist.
• The waist will feel too big before you have inserted the elastic.

Shown with the basic tube top (page 104).

Normannsgata

Sizes:	XS(S:M:L:XL)
Approx. measurements:	The waist measurement is made to fit using wide elastic. Use the size based on your hip measurement, measuring the broadest point around the hips: 103(112:122:131:140)cm / 40½(44:48:51½:55)in; Length: 76(78:80:82:84)cm / 30(30¾:31½:32¼:33)in
Suggested yarn:	Rauma Pelini
Yarn amount:	10(12:14:15:16) balls of 50g/102m/111yd balls of Rauma Pelini, DK (8-ply/ light worsted) yarn
Tension:	13 sts to 10cm (4in) square in stocking (stockinette) st using 7mm (UK 2, US 10½/11) needles
Suggested needles:	6mm (UK 4, US 10) and 7mm (UK 2, US 10½/11) circular needles
Extras:	5cm (2in) wide elastic for waistband casing. The length should be your waist measurement minus 5cm (2in). The elastic should be a similar colour to the chosen yarn

Cast on 94(106:118:130:142) sts using 2 strands of yarn on a 6mm (UK 4, US 10) circular needle. Place a marker at start of round and after 52(58:64:70:76) sts. It is a good idea for the markers to be the same colour. Knit 10 rounds. Purl 1 round, which will form folded edge at top. Knit another 10 rounds.

For best result, knit down edge now to form a casing. Remember to leave 4–5 sts open by the marker at the start so you can thread the elastic in at the end. Alternatively, sew the casing down at the end.

Change to a 7mm (UK 2, US 10½/11) circular needle. On round 1, inc 10 sts divided evenly until you have 104(116:128:140:152) sts. Place a marker after 26(29:32:35:38) sts and one 26(29:32:35:38) sts before end of round. These mark the sides so it is a good idea for these markers to be a different colour from the other two. Work 2 more rounds in stocking (stockinette) st. Now cont working in the round while increasing at side markers. More sts are increased at the back than at the front as foll:

Knit to 1 st before side marker, m1 right. Knit to next side marker. Knit 1 st past marker and m1 left.

Work 2 rounds in stocking (stockinette) st.

Knit to 1 st before side marker, m1 right. Knit 2 sts. M1 left. Knit until 1 st before next marker, m1 right, k2, m1 left.

Work 2 rounds in stocking (stockinette) st.

Rep rounds as described above until you have worked a total of 10 inc rounds and have 134(146:158:170:182) sts.

Inc for crotch: knit until work measures 28(29:30:31:32)cm / 11(11½:11¾:12¼:12½)in from folded top edge. Now inc for crotch at centre back marker. *Work to 2 sts past back marker, m1 left. Work until 2 sts before back marker, m1 right.*

Rep between * and * on every alt round, three times in total. On next round, rep increases at front and back, so you have increased four times at the back and once at the front. 144(156:168:180:192) sts.

On next round, cast (bind) off 4 sts at front and back, 2 sts before marker and 2 sts after marker. Place sts for one leg on a st holder or waste yarn. You should have approx. 68(74:80:86:92) sts per leg.

Place marker at inside leg. Work in the round and m1 before marker and m1 after marker on every alt round, three times in total.

Leg: knit until work measures 44(45:46:47:48)cm / 17¼(17¾18:18½:19)in from division for legs or to desired length. Work i-cord cast off as described below.

I-cord: cast on 2 extra sts at end of next round. Turn and work as foll: k1, slip next 2 sts loosely one by one, place them back on left-hand needle and k2tog tbl. Slip the 2 sts on right-hand needle back onto left-hand needle. Rep until 2 sts rem on needle. K2tog.

Rep for other leg.

Sew together at crotch and insert wide elastic in the casing at upper edge so the waist fits well.

Weave in all loose ends.

#midtsommerkulott #midsummerculottes #witredesign

BREEZY SUMMER TOP

The breezy summer top is perfect for a hot summer's day, worn over a dress to cover your shoulders, or with a high-waisted skirt or trousers. It is worked from the bottom up, has a side split and the back is slightly longer than the front. Stitches are picked up for very short sleeves and a ribbed neckband. And if you would prefer the top to be longer, feel free to knit it to the length of your choice.

Sizes:	XS(S:M:L–XL)
Approx. measurements:	Chest: 78(88:98:108)cm / 30¾(34¾:38½:42½)in;
	Length: 40(42:45:48)cm / 15¾(16½:17¾:19)in measured from front
Suggested yarn:	Rauma Petunia
Yarn amount:	4(5:6:7) balls of 50g/110m/120yd Rauma Petunia, DK (8-ply/light worsted)
Tension:	12 sts to 10cm (4in) square in stocking (stockinette) st using
	8mm (UK 0, US 11) needles
Suggested needles:	7mm (UK 2, US 10½/11) and 8mm (UK 0, US 11) circular needles

Cast on 45(51:57:63) sts using 2 strands of yarn on a 7mm (UK 2, US 10½/11) circular needle. Work 4 rows back and forth in k1, p1 rib for front. Knit sts onto an 8mm (UK 0, US 11) circular needle and set aside.

Cast on 45(51:57:63) sts on a 7mm (UK 2, US 10½/11) circular needle. Work 4 rows back and forth in k1, p1 rib for back. Knit onto an 8mm (UK 0, US 11) circular needle and work another 4 rows back and forth in stocking (stockinette) st.

Knit both sections together in stocking (stockinette) st in the round. On round 2: make 2 sts at each of the joins – 94(106:118:130) sts – and place a marker between these sts to mark position of armholes. Cont in stocking (stockinette) st in the round until work measures 22(24:26:29)cm / 8¾(9½:10¼11½)in measured from the front.

Front: place a marker at centre front. Work back and forth across front in stocking (stockinette) st until work measures 31(33:36:40)cm / 12¼(13:14¼:15¾)in. On next RS row, cast (bind) off centre 13(13:15:17) sts for neck or place on a st holder or waste yarn.

Cont working left side and dec 1 st at neck edge on every row, six times in total. 11(14:16:18) sts. Work until work measures 40(42:45:48)cm / 15¾(16½:17¾:19)in. Place rem sts on a st holder or waste yarn.

Work right side, and dec 1 st at neck edge on every row, six times in total. 11(14:16:18) sts. Work to same length as other side. Place rem sts on a st holder or waste yarn.

Back: work back to same length as front. Graft sts on front to same number of sts on back.

Leave rem sts for neck on needle.

Neckband: pick up sts around front neck using a 7mm (UK 2, US 10½/11) circular needle and knit sts for back neck onto needle. 60(66:72:78) sts. Work 4 rounds in k1, p1 rib. Cast (bind) off, remember to check the neck is stretchy enough.

Sleeves: pick up approx. 48(52:56:60) sts around armhole using an 8mm (UK 0, US 11) circular needle. Cast (bind) off on round 1; remember to check it is tight enough. Rep for other sleeve.

Weave in all loose ends. Hand-sew a couple of sts around the neck with yarn if there are any holes.

#luftigsommertopp
#breezysummertop
#witredesign

RETRO BUTTON TOP

The retro button top is inspired by an old knitted top I found in a second-hand shop. I imagine that tops like this had their heyday in around the 1970s, and spent their whole summers at festival after festival. So let's give it a new, long summer to enjoy! The top is worked back and forth from the bottom up. It is cropped and works well with high-waisted jeans or skirts, or over a summer dress.

Sizes:	XS(S:M:L:XL)
Approx. measurements:	Chest: 76(86:96:106:116)cm / 30(33¾:37¾:41¾:45½)in;
	Length: 41(43:46:50:54)cm / 16¼(17:18:19¾:21¼)in
Suggested yarn:	Rauma Pelini
Yarn amount:	3(4:4:5:6) balls of 50g/102m/111yd Rauma Pelini, DK (8-ply/light worsted) yarn
Tension:	20 sts and 23 rounds to 10cm (4in) square over stocking (stockinette) st using
	4mm (UK 8, US 6) needles
Suggested needles:	4mm (UK 8, US 6) circular needle and 3.5 (UK 10/9, US 4) circular needle for moss st edging

Cast on 148(168:188:208:228) sts on a 4mm (UK 8, US 6) circular needle. Work in moss st. Row 1: k1, p1 to end of row. Row 2: knit purl sts, and purl knit sts. Rep for 4 rows in total. Change to stocking (stockinette) st. Place a marker after 37(42:47:52:57) sts and 37(42:47:52:57) sts before end of row. Work back and forth until work measures 23(25:27:30:33)cm / 9(9¾:10¾:11¾:13)in. On next RS row, cast (bind) off 2 sts before marker and 2 sts after marker = 4 sts cast (bound) off at each marker.

Left front: turn and purl back the other way to armhole. Turn and k1, k2tog, knit to end of row. Rep these two rows until work measures 26(28:30:33:36)cm / 10¼(11:11¾:13:14¼)in. On next WS row, cast (bind) off 10(12:14:16:18) sts at neck edge. Cont in stocking (stockinette) st. Dec as before at armhole on each RS row and at the same time dec at neck as foll: work to last 3 sts, k2tog tbl, k1. Rep decreases = 2 sts dec on each RS row until 9(9:11:13:13) sts rem on needle. Work until work measures 41(43:46:50:54)cm / 16¼(17:18:19¾:21¼)in. Place sts on a st holder or waste yarn.

Back: work back and forth in stocking (stockinette) st over the 70(80:90:100:110) sts for back. On every RS row: k1, k2tog. Knit to end of row to last 3 sts, k2tog tbl, k1. Rep dec row on RS 10(12:14:16:18) times until you have 50(56:62:68:74) sts on needle. Cont without decreasing until work measures 36(38:40:43:46)cm / 14½(15:15¾:17:18)in. On next RS row, cast (bind) off centre 24(26:28:30:32) sts for neck. Cont on left side of back. On every RS row: dec for neck as foll: k1, k2tog, knit to end of row. Dec as set until 9(9:11:13:13) sts rem on needle. Cont without decreasing until back is same length as front.

Graft straps on left side together, or cast (bind) off and sew together at shoulders. Rep on right side of back. On every RS row: knit to last 3 sts, k2tog tbl, k1. Dec as set until 9(9:11:13:13) sts rem on needle. Work to same length as left side.

Right front: start at neck edge. Work in stocking (stockinette) st to last 3 sts, k2tog tbl, k1. Rep decreases on every RS row until work measures 26(28:30:33:36) cm / 10¼(11:11¾:13:14¼)in. On next RS row, cast (bind) off 10(12:14:16:18) sts from neck edge. Cont in stocking (stockinette) st, decreasing as before at armhole and at the same time decreasing at neck as foll: k1, k2tog. Rep decreases = 2 sts dec on each RS row, until 9(9:11:13:13) sts rem on needle. Cont without decreasing until work measures 41(43:46:50:54)cm / 16¼(8¾(17:18:19¾:21¼)in.

Graft straps together; or straps can be cast (bound) off and sewn together.

Moss st neckband: start with the cast (bound) off sts on right side. Using a 3.5mm (UK 9/10, US 4) circular needle, pick up approx. 90(100:110:120:130) sts around front neck, back of neck and cast (bound) off sts at left front neck. Work 3 rows of moss st in total as shown for start of body. Cast (bind) off in moss st (knit purl sts and purl knit sts). Check as you go that the cast-(bind-)off edge feels tight enough. It should be stretchy but sufficiently tight that it does not sag at the front.

Moss st button bands: pick up approx. 45(48:52:56:60) sts down left front. Work in moss st as before for 3 rows in total. Cast (bind) off in moss st (knit purl sts and purl knit sts). Check as you go that the cast-(bind-)off edge feels tight enough. Pick up same number of sts along right front. Work 1 row in moss st. Mark where you want buttonholes; approx. 6–8 buttonholes, evenly spaced. Turn, work moss st while making buttonholes: sl1, k2tog at markers. Work 1 row in moss st = 3 rows in total. Cast (bind) off in moss st (knit purl sts and purl knit sts). Check as you go that the cast-(bind-)off edge feels tight enough.

Edge armholes in moss st: pick up approx. 65(70:75:80:85) sts around armhole. Work in moss st as before, in the round, for 3 rows in total. Cast (bind) off in moss st (knit purl sts and purl knit sts). Rep for other sleeve.

Weave in all loose ends and sew on buttons.

#retroknappetopp #retrobuttontop #witredesign

NORDIC SUMMER DRESS

The Nordic summer dress is a simple, basic A-line dress. It is quite wide and is knitted from the bottom up using two strands of cotton/linen yarn. The dress might feel heavy when on the needles but it hangs attractively and is snug and cool when worn. You could wear it with a belt, or knit an i-cord to go round the waist. It looks good and will prevent the dress from sagging.

Sizes:	XS(S:M:L:XL)
Approx. measurements:	Circumference around bottom edge: 108(117:130:138:148)cm / 42½(46:51:54¼:58¼)in;
	Chest under armholes: 77(86:98:108:117)cm / 30¼(33¾:38½:42½:46)in;
	Length including strap: 84(87:90:93:96)cm / 33(34¼:35½:36½:37¾)in
Suggested yarn:	Rauma Petunia
Yarn amount:	9(10:12:14:16) balls of 50g/110m/120yd Rauma Petunia, DK (8-ply/light worsted) yarn
Tension:	13 sts and 17 rows to 10cm (4in) square over stocking (stockinette) st
Suggested needles:	7mm (UK 2, US 10½/11) circular needle

Cast on 140(152:168:180:192) sts using 2 strands of yarn on a 7mm (UK 2, US 10½/11) circular needle. Place a marker at start of round and another after 70(76:84:90:96) sts. These mark the sides of the dress. Work in stocking (stockinette) st until work measures 20(22:24:25:27)cm / 7¾(8¾:9½:9¾:10¾)in. Now dec down sides evenly. *Work to 1 st after marker, k2tog. Work to 3 sts before next marker, k2tog tbl*. Rep between * and * at both markers, every 6(7:7:8:8) rounds, ten times in total = 40 sts decreased. Cont in stocking (stockinette) st until work measures 61(63:65:67:69)cm / 24(24¾:25½:26½:27¼) in. For sizes M, L and XL, dec 2 sts before marker and 2 sts after marker = 4 sts dec at both markers. For sizes XS and S there are no underarm decreases. 100(112:120:132:144) sts.

Front: work across front until last 2 sts, k2tog. Turn, purl back the other way to last 2 sts at other underarm, p2tog. Remember to always slip first st off loosely. Rep five times in total on each side, for 10 rows in total. Place a marker at the centre front.

On next RS row, work to marker at centre front and cast (bind) off 5(6:7:8:9) sts neatly. Cont to armhole until last 2 sts. *k2tog at end of row as before. Turn, purl back until last 2 sts before neck, k2tog*. Rep from * to * once more. Continue to dec at neck edge on every alt row, but only dec every alt time at armhole, i.e. on every fourth row. Rep until 3 sts rem on needle. Work in stocking (stockinette) st for 2(3:3:4:4)cm / ¾(1¼:1¼:1½:1½)in or to desired length. Measure dress against the wearer. Place sts on a spare needle or waste yarn.

Join yarn at centre front on WS. Cast (bind) off 5(6:7:8:9) sts neatly. Rep shapings as described above.

Back: make back the same way as described for front. For the neatest result, graft straps together, or cast (bind) off and sew together at shoulders

Sew a stitch to reinforce at underarm. Weave in all loose ends.

#nordisksommerkjole #nordicsummerdress #witredesign

Tips

• *All bodies are different. It is a good idea to measure the knitting against the wearer as you go along.*

• *Remember to check your tension.*

• *The stitches at the neck and armhole will not be picked up for a neckband or sleeve once the dress is finished. This means that it is important to work edge stitches as knit stitches for a neat result. Always slip first stitch off loosely with yarn in the front or at the back of work depending on whether you are on RS or WS.*

• *The back and front of the dress look identical.*

NORDIC SUMMER TOP

The Nordic summer top is a simple yet elegant top for everyday wear or special occasions. It is knitted from the bottom up using two strands of yarn on big needles. The top is snug, made in thick yarn, which also means it hangs well, and it looks great with high-waisted skirts or trousers.

Sizes:	XS(S:M:L–XL)
Approx. measurements:	Chest: 77(87:97:107)cm / 30¼(34¼:38¼:42¼)in;
	Length: 46(48:51:54)cm / 18(19:20:21¼)in
Suggested yarn:	Rauma Petunia
Yarn amount:	4(4:5:6) balls of 50g/110m/120yd Rauma Petunia,
	DK (8-ply/light worsted) yarn
Tension:	12 sts and 15 rows to 10cm (4in) square over stocking
	(stockinette) st
Suggested needles:	8mm (UK 0, US 11) circular needle

Cast on 92(104:116:128) sts using 2 strands of yarn on an 8mm (UK 0, US 11) circular needle. Place a marker at start of round and one after 46(52:58:64) sts. These mark the armholes. Work in stocking (stockinette) st in the round until work measures 25(27:30:33)cm / 9¾(10¾:11¾:13)in.

Divide for front and back: place a new marker at centre front. Work to last 2 sts before marker at armhole and k2tog. Turn and purl back the other way. Work to last 2 sts before other armhole marker and p2tog. Slip first st loosely for a neat edge. Rep five times in total on each side, for 10 rows in total.

Work to marker at centre front and cast (bind) off 5 sts neatly. Cont towards armhole until last 2 sts,* k2tog at end of row as before. Turn, purl back until last 2 sts before neck, k2tog*. Rep from * to * once more. Continue to work dec at neck as set, but only dec at armhole every alt time, i.e. every fourth row. Rep until 3 sts rem on needle. Work 4(4:5:6)cm / 1½(1½:2:2¼)in stocking (stockinette) st or to desired length. Place sts on a spare needle or waste yarn.

Rejoin yarn at centre front from WS. Cast (bind) off 5 sts neatly. Make back the same way as described for front.

For the neatest result, graft straps together, or cast (bind) off and sew together at shoulders. Weave in all loose ends and press/block the bottom edge to prevent it rolling up.

#nordisksommertopp #nordicsummertop #witredesign

Tips

• *All bodies are different. It is a good idea to measure the knitting against the wearer as you go along.*

• *Remember to check your tension.*

• *The stitches at neck and armhole will not be picked up for a neckband or sleeve. This means that it is important to work edge stitches as knit stitches for a neat result. Always slip first stitch off loosely. If the previous row was a knit row, the yarn must be at the front. If the previous row was a purl row, the yarn must be at the back.*

• *The front and back of the top look identical.*

Autumn

RETRO BUTTON DRESS

The retro button dress is inspired by the 1970s, perfect for wearing with bare legs and a flower crown. It is knee length and narrows up to the waist. The dress is knitted in the round, bottom up. This means that one button band is knitted together with the rest of the dress. Stitches are picked up along the button band at the end to create buttonholes. So, although it looks as though the dress is knitted back and forth, there is no need to worry about buttons coming undone on hot summer days.

Sizes:	XS(S:M:L)
Approx. measurements:	Circumference around bottom edge: 102(109:115:122)cm / 40¼(43:45¼:48)in;
	Chest under armholes: 76(86:96:106)cm / 30(33¾:37¾:41¾)in;
	Length: 103(105:107:109)cm / 40½(41½:42¼:43)in
Suggested yarn:	Rauma Pelini
Yarn amount:	9(10:11:12) balls of 50g/102m/111yd Rauma Pelini, DK (8-ply/light worsted) yarn
Tension:	20 sts to 10cm (4in) square in stocking (stockinette) st using 4mm (UK 8, US 6) needles
Suggested needles:	4mm (UK 8, US 6) circular needle and 3.5 (UK 10/9, US 4) circular needle for moss st edging
Extras:	10–12 buttons

Body: Cast on 204(217:230:243) sts on a 4mm (UK 8, US 6) circular needle. Work in moss st as follows: Round 1: k1, p1 to end of round. Round 2: purl knit sts and knit purl sts. Rep for 4 rounds in total and change to stocking (stockinette) st. Place marker at start of round, which here will be at centre front of dress. Remember that the 2 sts before and after marker must always be worked in moss st to form button band. Work in stocking (stockinette) st in the round until work measures 38(40:42:44)cm / 15(15¾:16½:17¼)in.

Now start to dec to make dress narrower towards waist: dec 8(7:6:5) sts evenly around round every 4cm (1½in). Mark with markers to make sure the decreases come in the same place on each round. Rep seven times in total. 148(168:188:208) sts. Place a marker after 37(42:47:52) sts and 37(42:47:52) sts before end of round. These mark the armholes. Cont in the round until work measures 86(87:88:89)cm / 33¾(34¼:34¾:35)in or desired length to armholes. Dec 2 sts before and 2 sts after markers at armholes = 4 sts dec on both sides.

Front: work back and forth across front while decreasing at armholes on each RS row as foll: k1, k2tog. Work to end of round to last 3 sts, k2tog tbl, k1. Purl back the other way. Rep these 2 rows for 3cm (1¼in) from armhole. On next RS row, cast (bind) off centre 20(24:28:32) sts incl moss st sts.

Right side of front: cont decreasing at armhole as before, while decreasing for neck as foll: k1, k2tog. Rep decreases until 9(9:11:13) sts rem on needle. Cont without decreasing until work measures 18(18:19:20)cm / 7(7:7½:7¾)in from armhole. Place sts on a st holder or waste yarn.

Left side of front: start at armhole. Work to last 3 sts, k2tog tbl, k1 and dec as previously for armhole. Rep on each RS row until 9(9:11:13) sts rem on needle. Cont until work measures the same length as right side of front.

Continued overleaf.

Back: work back and forth in stocking (stockinette) st over the 70(80:90:100) sts for back. On every RS row: k1, k2tog. Knit to end of row to last 3 sts. k2tog tbl, k1. Rep dec row from RS 10(12:14:16) times until 50(56:62:68) sts rem on needle. Cont without decreasing until work measures 13(13:14:15)cm / 5(5:5½:6)in from armhole. On next RS row, cast (bind) off centre 24(26:28:30) sts for neck. Cont on left side of back. Dec for neck on each RS row as foll: k1, k2tog, knit to end of row. Cont decreasing as set until 9(9:11:13) sts rem on needle. Cont without decreasing until back is same length as front. Graft straps on left side together, or cast (bind) off and sew together at shoulders.

Rep on right side of back. On every RS row: knit to last 3 sts, k2tog tbl, k1. Dec as set until 9(9:11:13) sts rem on needle. Work to same length as left side. Graft straps on right side together. Or cast (bind) off and sew together at shoulders.

Moss st neckband: start at centre of moss st button band at centre front. Using a 3.5mm (UK 9/10, US 4) circular needle, pick up approx. 90(100:110:120) sts all the way around neck. Work 3 rows of moss st in total as shown for start of body. Cast (bind) off in moss st. Check as you go that the cast (bound) off edge feels tight enough. It should be stretchy but still sufficiently tight that the dress does not sag at the front.

Moss st button band: starting at the bottom, pick up approx. 20 sts per 10cm (4in) along right side of band using a 3.5mm (UK 9/10, US 4) circular needle. Work 2 rows in moss st. Mark where you want buttonholes using markers; mark approx. 10–12 buttonholes, evenly spaced. Cont in moss st while making buttonholes: sl1, k2tog at marker. Work 1 row in moss st = 4 rows in total. Cast (bind) off in moss st: knit purl sts and purl knit sts. Check as you go that the cast-(bind-)off edge feels tight enough.

Armhole edging in moss st: using a 3.5mm (UK 9/10, US 4) circular needle, pick up approx. 65(70:75:80) sts around armhole. Work in moss st as before, in the round, for 3 rows in total. Cast (bind) off in moss st: knit purl sts and purl knit sts. Cast (bind) off. Rep for other sleeve.

Weave in all loose ends and sew on buttons.

#retroknappekjole #retrobuttondress #witredesign

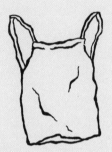

NORTH WEST TOP

The North West top is a cool top with simple detailing. It is knitted from the bottom up and has a folded edge at the top on the front and back for a sharp finish. The straps are worked as i-cords so the length can be easily adjusted to fit. The top will feel roomier than the measurements on the next page indicate as the straps sit mostly on the upper back, and do not cover the whole upper body. It is therefore recommended that you choose a size 2cm (¾in) smaller than your own chest measurement.

Sizes:	XS(S:M:L:XL)
Approx. measurements:	Chest: 76(84:92:100:108)cm / 30(33:36¼:39½:42½)in; Length: 41(44:47:50:53)cm / 16¼(17¼:18½:19¾:20¾)in
Suggested yarn:	Rauma Petunia
Yarn amount:	3(4:4:5:5) balls of 50g /110m/120yd Rauma Petunia, DK (8-ply/light worsted) yarn
Tension:	20 sts to 10cm (4in) square over stocking (stockinette st) using 4mm (UK 8, US 6) needles
Suggested needles:	4mm (UK 8, US 6) and 3mm (UK 11, US 2/3) circular needle
Extras:	Sewing needle and threads

Cast on 152(168:184:200:216) sts on a 4mm (UK 8, US 6) circular needle. Place a marker at start of round and another after 76(84:99:100:108) sts. These mark the armholes. Work in stocking (stockinette) st in the round until work measures 26(28:30:32:34)cm / 10¼(11:11¾:12½:13½)in. Now work front and back separately. Move the sts on the part you are not working onto another needle, if you prefer.

Tips
• All bodies are different. It is a good idea to measure the knitting against the wearer as you go along.
• Remember to check your tension.
• The stitches at the armhole will not be picked up. This means that it is important to work edge stitches as knit stitches for an attractive result. Always slip first st off loosely. If the previous row was a knit row, the yarn must be at the front. If the previous row was a purl row, the yarn must be at the back.

Front: work 2cm (¾in) back and forth across front in stocking (stockinette) st. Cont in stocking (stockinette) st and k2tog at the end of each row. Always slip first st off loosely with yarn in front of work to create a knit edge st. Cont as set until you have decreased 16(18:20:22:24) times on each side in total and 44(48:52:56:60) sts rem on needle. Change to a 3mm (UK 11, US 2/3) circular needle and work 2cm (¾in) in stocking (stockinette) st over rem sts. Purl 1 row to mark the fold line and work 2cm (¾in) in stocking (stockinette) st. Cast (bind) off while knitting down folded edge or cast (bind) off and sew edge down neatly.

Back: knit sts for back onto 3mm (UK 11, US 2/3) needle and dec 10 sts evenly across first row. Work 2cm (¾in) back and forth in stocking (stockinette) st. Purl 1 row to mark the fold line and work 2cm (¾in) in stocking (stockinette) st. Cast (bind) off while knitting down folded edge or cast (bind) off and sew edge down neatly.

i-cord straps: using a 4mm circular needle (UK 8, US 6), pick up 2 sts at one corner of front. Work i-cord to desired length, approx. 25cm (9¾in). Cast (bind) off and attach cord neatly to back, approx. 10–15cm (4–6in) in from armhole. Rep on other side of front and attach cord to other side of back.

Sew together where folded edge on back meets the 2cm (¾in) in stocking (stockinette) st on front under arms using mattress st. Weave in all loose ends. Firmly press edges and hem with a sewing needle and thread.

#northwesttop #witredesign

BREEZY SUMMER DRESS

The breezy summer dress is a dress with light, airy stitches. It goes down to around the knees and stretches to about 5cm (2in) longer than the stated measurements when worn. The dress works perfectly for the beach or anywhere you might want to be on a hot summer's day, but depending on where that is, you might want to wear something underneath it, such as a shirt, if the weather is cooler. The dress may be more suited to warmer climes but it also fits in perfectly with the nature here on Engeløya!

It is worked from the bottom up, has short side splits and the back is slightly longer than the front. Stitches are picked up for very short sleeves that skim the shoulders; and the dress also has a ribbed neckband.

Sizes:	XS(S:M:L:XL)
Approx. measurements:	Circumference around bottom edge: 98(108:118:128:138)cm / 38½(42½:46½ 50¼:54¼)in;
	Chest under armholes: 78(88:98:108:118)cm / 30¾(34¾:38½:42½:46½)in;
	Total length: 89(91:93:95:95)cm / 35(35¾:36½:37½:37½)in measured from front
Suggested yarn:	Rauma Petunia
Yarn amount:	10(12:13:15:19) balls of 50g/110m/120yd Rauma Petunia, DK (8-ply/light worsted) yarn
Tension:	12 sts to 10cm (4in) square over stocking (stockinette) st using 8mm (UK 0, US 11) needles
Suggested needles:	7mm (UK 2, US 10½/11) and 8mm (UK 0, US 11) circular needles

Front: Cast on 57(63:69:75:81) sts using 2 strands of yarn on a 7mm (UK 2, US 10½/11) circular needle. Work 4 rows back and forth in k1, p1 rib. Knit sts onto an 8mm (UK 0, US 11) circular needle and set work aside.

Back: cast on 57(63:69:75:81) sts on a 7mm (UK 2, US 10½/11) circular needle. Work 4 rows back and forth in k1, p1 rib. Knit onto an 8mm (UK 0, US 11) circular needle and work another 8 rows back and forth in stocking (stockinette) st.

Knit both sections together in stocking (stockinette) st in the round. On round 2, make 2 sts at each of the joins = 118(130:142:154:166) sts – and place a marker between these sts to mark armholes. Cont to work stocking (stockinette) st in the round until work measures 32(34:36:38:38)cm / 12½(13½:14¼:15:15)in measured from the front.

Now start to dec to make dress narrower towards waist. Dec 6 sts evenly across round, placing markers at decreases. Rep decreases every 5cm (2in) four times in total. 94(106:118:130:142) sts. Cont to work stocking (stockinette) st in the round until work measures 71(72:73:74:74)cm / 28(28¼:28¾:29¼:29¼)in measured from the front and you are ready to dec for armholes and neck.

Fronts: place a marker at centre front. Work back and forth across front until work measures 81(82:83:84:85)cm / 32(32¼:32¾:33:33½)in. On next RS row, cast (bind) off centre 13(13:15:17:17) sts for neck or place on a st holder or waste yarn. Cont working left side of front and dec 1 st at neck edge on every row, six times in total. 11(14:16:18:21) sts. Cont until work measures 89(91:93:95:95)cm / 35(35¾:36½:37½:37½)in. Place rem sts on a st holder or waste yarn.

Start at armhole on right side and cast (bind) off 1 st at neck edge on every row, six times in total. 11(14:16:18:21) sts. Work until work measures same length as left side of front. Place rem sts on a st holder or waste yarn.

Back: work back to same length as fronts. Graft sts on fronts to same number of sts on each side of back. Leave rem sts for neck on needle.

Neckband: pick up around neck on a 7mm (UK 2, US 10½/11) circular needle and knit sts for neck onto needle. 60(66:72:78:80) sts. Work 4 rounds in k1, p1 rib. Cast (bind) off, remembering to check the neck is stretchy enough.

Sleeves: using an 8mm (UK 0, US 11) circular needle, pick up 48(52:56:60:64) sts around armhole. Cast (bind) off on round 1. Remember to check cast-(bind-)off edge is tight enough. Rep for other sleeve. Weave in all loose ends and add a couple of sts around the neck if there are holes.

#luftigsommerkjole
#breezysummerdress
#witredesign

Tips
• All bodies are different. It is a good idea to measure the knitting against the wearer as you go along.
• Remember to check your tension.
• Add markers when decreasing evenly around the dress so the decreases come in the same place on each round.
• For more information on how to graft shoulders, search for videos on 'grafting stocking (stockinette) stitch' or 'Kitchener stitch' online.

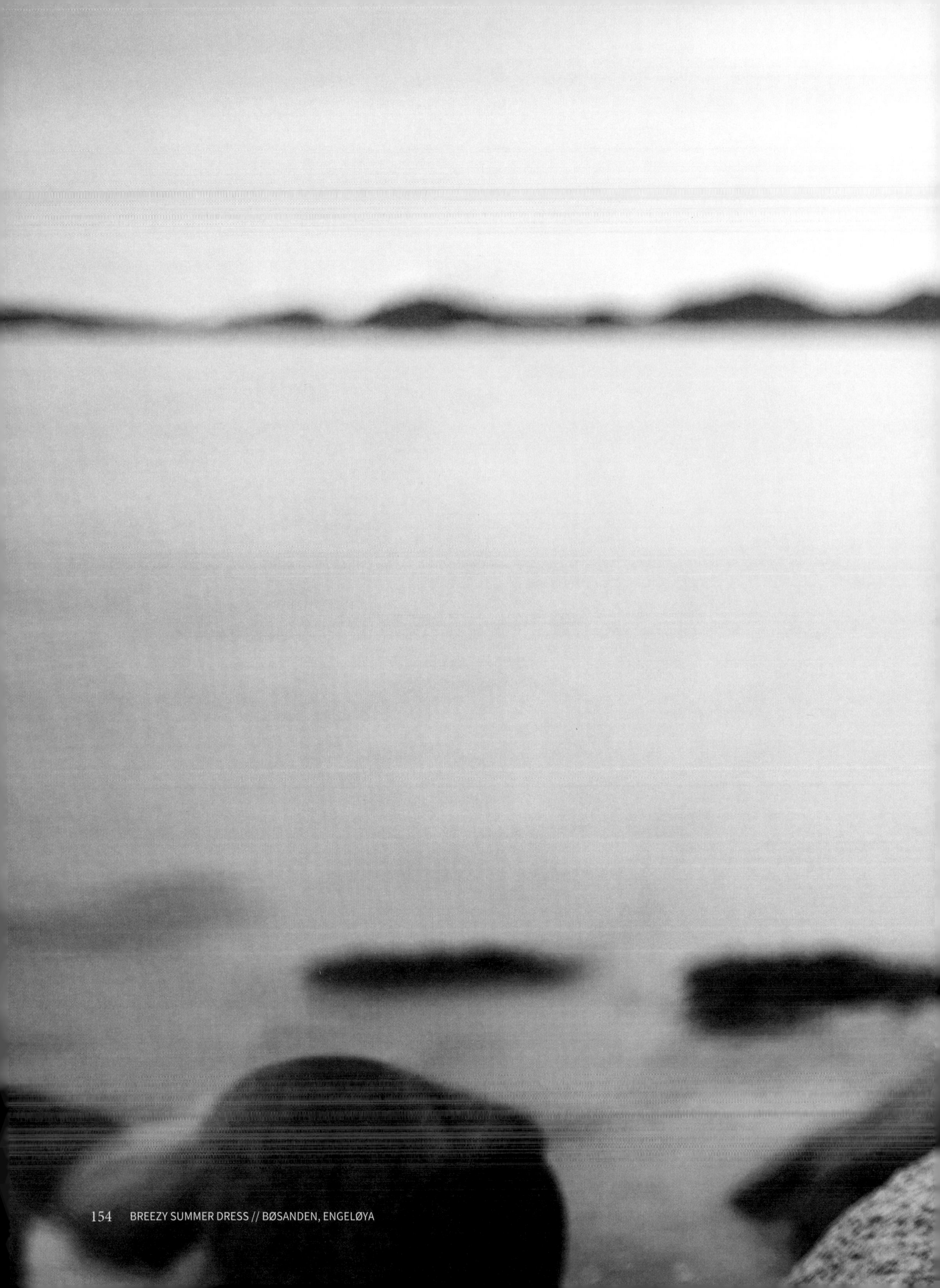

COLLETT JACKET

The Collett jacket is a jacket with attractive shoulder detailing and a narrow, semi-high neck. It is knitted flat from the top down in one strand of 5-ply (sport weight) yarn and two strands of 1–3-ply (lace weight). First, stitches are increased for the body to produce the attractive shoulder detail, before going on to increase for both the body and the sleeves at the same time. The jacket is finished off with short rows at the bottom to make it a little longer at the back than the front before the rib. The start of the button bands is worked at the same time as the neck at the top and then placed on a spare needle while you work the jacket itself. The button band is then worked separately and attached afterwards. The jacket can be adapted to be shorter or longer as it can be tried on as you work.

COLLETT JACKET // FONN-HOLAND FARM, ENGELØYA   157

Sizes:	XS(S:M:L:XL)
Approx. measurements:	Chest: 96(104:111:119:126)cm / 37¾(41:43¼:46¾:49½)in;
	Length at centre front 52(55:58:61:64)cm / 20¾(21¼:22¾:24:25¼)in
Suggested yarns:	Rauma Finull and Rauma Plum
Yarn amount:	5(5:6:6:6) balls of 50g/175m/191yd Rauma Finull, 5-ply (sport) yarn; 7(7:8:9:9)
	balls of 25g/250m/273yd Rauma Plum, 1–3-ply (lace) yarn
Tension:	16 sts to 10cm (4in) in stocking (stockinette) st on a 4.5mm (UK 7, US 7) needle;
	20 sts to 10cm (4in) in rib on a 3.5mm (UK 9/10, US 4) needle
Suggested needles:	3.5mm (UK 9/10, US 4) and 4.5mm (UK 7, US 7) circular needles
Extras:	Seven to nine buttons, depending on size

Cast on 83(91:99:107:115) sts on a 3.5mm (UK 9/10, US 4) circular needle using 1 strand of Finull and 2 strands of Plum. (The neck, which you are casting on for now, consists of button bands of 11 sts each on either side.) Work back and forth in rib as foll: k1 (edge st), k1, p1 and end with k1, k1 (edge st). Turn and cont in rib. When neck measures 3cm (1¼in), make first buttonhole from WS as foll: work 4 sts in rib as set, cast (bind) off 2 sts and cont in rib to end of row. On next row, cast on 2 sts where you cast (bind) off for buttonhole. Work in rib until neckband measures 5cm (2in). On last row of rib, add a marker around sts 24+26(26:28:28+30:30+32: 32+34), counting in from both ends of row. You should now have 4 markers on your needle.

Change to a 4.5mm (UK 7, US 7) circular needle and place first and last 11 sts on a spare needle or waste yarn. These sts will be knitted as button bands once the body has been worked. Cast on 1 new st at start of row. Work raglan on each RS row at the same time as working short rows as described below:

Raglan (body only): inc for raglan on the outside of the 2 marked sts on each side. This means that the shoulder detail is created over 3 sts. The raglan increases are worked on every alt row by picking up the strand of yarn on the outside of the marked st and knitting into it (m1). While you are working the short rows, the raglan increases are also worked on every RS row. On right-hand side of marked st, m1 to right, on left-hand side, m1 to left. Inc five times in total at all markers.

Short rows for neck: work until you are 2 sts past last marker for right sleeve, turn and purl back the other way until you are 2 sts past last marker for left sleeve. Cont as set, turning 2 sts nearer to end of row each time. Turn five times each side in total. After last short row, m1 at end of row. You now have 81(89:97:105:113) sts on your needle + 2 extra sts and will now continue increasing for both body and sleeves at the same time.

Raglan (body and sleeves): at inside of the markers, inc for sleeves on every alt row as foll: work marked st, m1 to left. Work up to st before next marked st, m1 and twist to right. The new sts will thus be turned away from the marked st. At outside of marked sts, continue to inc as before. After 3 increases for sleeves and 8 increases for body in total, including previous increases, continue to inc for sleeves but inc for body on every fourth row only. 105(113:121:129:137) sts + 2 extra sts. Cont as described above, on every alt round for sleeves and every fourth round for body until you have increased for sleeves 24(26:28:30:32) times in total. 51(55:59:63:67) sts for each sleeve including marker st. Cont working across all sts but continue to inc for body on every round until you have increased for body 20(21:22:23:24) times in total (including increases at top shoulder). 237(257:277:297:317) sts + 2 extra sts.

On next round, place sts for sleeves, including marked raglan sts onto a st holder or waste yarn = 51(55:59:63:67) sts for each sleeve. Cast on 4 new sts at each side and place a marker in centre here. Cont to work in the round across all body sts = 143(155:167:179:191) sts plus 2 extra sts – until work measures 47(50:53:56:59)cm / 18½(19¾:20¾:22:23¼)in measured from under neckband at centre front. On last row, cast (bind) off the extra sts on each side of jacket. Work short rows at back as explained below:

Short rows for back, at bottom of body: work back until 5 sts before side marker. Turn and work until 5 sts before marker at other side. Turn and work until 15 sts before marker. Continue as set, 10 sts longer each time, until you have turned four times on each side in total. Work to centre back and break off yarn. Set work aside.

Button bands: place sts for left button band on a 3.5mm (UK 9/10, US 4) circular needle. Cast on 1 new st facing body. Work back and forth in rib pat as set + 1 new edge st, until button band measures same length as jacket. Cast (bind) off the extra st facing body on last row and move sts to the circular needle you have at the bottom.

Mark where you want buttonholes on your jacket on the left button band, approx. 6–8 buttonholes, depending on button size. Remember that there will be a buttonhole in the rib at the bottom that will be worked last.

Place sts for right button band on a 3.5mm (UK 9/10, US 4) circular needle. Cast on 1 new st facing body. Work back and forth in rib pat as set + 1 new edge st, and add buttonholes from WS in same way as before where marked: work 4 sts in rib as set, cast (bind) off 2 sts and cont in rib to end of row. On next row, cast on 2 sts where you cast (bind) off for buttonhole. Cont until button band measures same length as jacket and cast (bind) off extra st facing body on last row. Move sts to the circular needle you have at the bottom.

Attach button bands to jacket using mattress st inside the extra sts added on each side.

Work all sts at bottom of jacket on a 3.5mm (UK 9/10, US 4) circular needle in k1, p1 rib. After 2.5cm (1in), make last buttonhole from WS in the same way as before. Cont until rib measures 5cm (2in). Cast (bind) off in rib.

Sleeves: place sts for sleeve on a 4.5mm (UK 7, US 7) circular needle and pick up 4 new sts in the new sts added at the underarm. You now have a total of 55(59:63:67:71) sts on your needle. Place a marker at centre underarm. Cont in stocking (stockinette) st in the round, at the same time decreasing on either side of marker as foll: after marker, k2tog. Before marker k2tog tbl. Rep every 3.5cm (1⅜in), eight times in total until 39(43:47:51:55) sts rem on needle. Work until sleeve measures 39(40:41:42:42)cm / 15¼(15¾:16¼:16½:16½)in or to desired length. Change to a 3.5mm (UK 9/10, US 4) circular needle and dec 11 sts on round 1, while working k1, p1 rib for 5cm (2in) in total. Cast (bind) off in rib. Rep for other sleeve.

Weave in all loose ends. Press/block the raglan increases well, and press/block top of front and back so the jacket hangs well.

#collettjacket #witredesign

CHUNKY BRIOCHE SWEATER

The chunky brioche sweater is knitted flat in brioche stitch, using two strands of yarn on large needles. You cast on for the front and decrease for the neck before increasing again at the back of the neck and working downwards on the back. This means that there are no shoulder seams. The sides are then joined up to the armhole where stitches are picked up for the sleeves, which are knitted downwards to the desired length.

The sweater should be hand-rinsed and blocked flat to the desired shape before wear. This will help the stitches to settle and the sweater will then keep its shape. If you want a more compact sweater that is not blocked, it is best to go up a size.

Tips

• *All bodies are different. It is a good idea to measure the knitting against the wearer as you go along.*

• *Remember to check your tension. It is recommended to knit a swatch to check tension in stocking (stockinette) stitch.*

• *Brioche stitch can be tricky to measure. Place the garment flat and leave it for a while before measuring.*

• *For best results, the stocking (stockinette) stitch hem can be knitted down as you cast (bind) off. Search for 'cast-off hem for top-down knitting' (or 'knit a folded hem') online for more information.*

Sizes:	XS(S:M:L:XL)
Approx. measurements:	Chest: 100(112:123:134:146)cm / 39½(44:48½:52¾:57½)in;
	Length: 44(47:50:53:56)cm / 17¼(18½:19¾:20¾:22)in
Suggested yarn:	Hip Wool
Yarn amount:	12(14:16:18:20) balls of 50g/80m/87yd Hip Wool, aran (10-ply/worsted) yarn
Tension:	7 sts to 10cm (4in) in brioche st and 9 sts to 10cm (4in) in stocking (stockinette) st
Suggested needles:	10mm (UK 000, US 15) circular needle

Cast on 35(39:43:47:51) sts using 2 strands of yarn on a 10mm (UK 2, US 10½/11) circular needle.

Set-up row: k1 (edge st). *k1, yfwd, s1 loosely purlwise*. Rep from * to *. End with k1 + k1 (edge st). Row 2: k1 (edge st). * yfwd, sl1 loosely purlwise. Knit next st and yfwd together*. Rep from * to *. End with yfwd, sl1 loosely purlwise + k1 (edge st).

Row 3: k1 (edge st). *Knit next st and yfwd together. yfwd, sl1 loosely purlwise*. Rep from * to *. End by knitting next st and yfwd together + k1 (edge st).

Rep rows 2 and 3 until work measures 37(39:41:43:45)cm / 14½(15¼:16¼:17:17¾)in. On next RS row, cast (bind) off centre 9(9:9:11:11) sts. Work to end of row.

Right front: work back again in brioche st as set to last two sts before neck edge, k2tog. Turn, k2tog at start of next row. Rep decreases on every row at neck edge 2(2:3:3:4) times in total. Work over the 11(13:14:15:16) sts on your needle until front measures 41(44:47:50:53)cm / 16¼(17¼:18½:19¾:20¾)in. Break yarn. Leave sts on needle or move to a st holder if preferred.

Left front: start at neck opening and work to end of row. Work back again in brioche st as set to last two sts before neck edge, k2tog. Turn, k2tog at start of next row. Rep decreases on every row at neck edge 2(2:3:3:4) times in total. Work over the 11(13:14:15:16) sts on your needle until front measures 41(44:47:50:53)cm / 16¼(17¼:18½:19¾:20¾)in. Do not break yarn.

Work to neck opening, cast on 13(13:15:17:19) sts at neck and cont across right front.

Back: cont in brioche patt as set until back is the same length as front. Cast off loosely.

Join front and back at sides, e.g. using mattress st for 22(24:26:28:30)cm / 8¾(9½:10¼:11:11¾)in up from the bottom. This will produce an armhole that is 19(20:21:22:23)cm / 7½(7¾:8¼:8¾:9)in deep.

Sleeves: pick up 29(31:33:35:37) sts around armhole. Sleeves are worked back and forth due to brioche st patt. Rep the set-up row + rows 2 and 3 at the start of the instructions. Work back and forth, and at the same time k2tog for first two and last two sts in row (these become a new edge st) every 8cm (3¼in), 3(3:3:4:4) times in total = 6(6:6:8:8) sts decreased. Cont straight until sleeve measures 38(39:40:41:42)cm / 15(15¼:15¾:16¼:16½)in.

Cuff: change to stocking (stockinette) st, work in the round if preferred, and dec down to 20(21:22:23:24) sts on first row. Work 9 rows in stocking (stockinette) st. Cast (bind) off and sew edge down. Or for best result, knit folded edge down as you cast (bind) off. Rep for other sleeve.

Neckband: pick up 1 st in the 'knit' sts and 2 sts in the 'purl' sts evenly around neck opening = 44(44:46:48:50) sts. Work 12 rows in stocking (stockinette) st. Cast (bind) off and sew edge down. Or for best result, knit folded edge down as you cast (bind) off. Remember to check it is stretchy enough.

Bottom hem: pick up 1 st in the 'knit' sts and alternate 1 st and 2 sts in the 'purl' sts = 90(95:100:105:110) sts. If necessary dec down to correct number of sts on first round. Work 9 rounds in stocking (stockinette) st. For best result, knit folded edge down as you cast (bind) off, or cast (bind) off and sew down.

Sew sleeve seams. Weave in all loose ends.

#chunkypatentgenser #chunkybriochesweater #witredesign

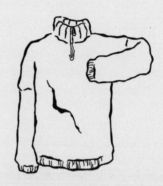

MEN'S URBAN POLAR SWEATER

The urban polar sweater is a soft, warm sweater, knitted using a combination of two different yarns on large needles. It works well in town, going to or from work, in the forest or out at sea. The neckband is doubled over in rib, making a snug and close-fitting neckline that is not too tight. The zip is practical but is also an eye-catching detail. The sweater is knitted from the bottom up. The zip is sewn in by hand with one strand of chunky (bulky) yarn. Stitches are picked up for the sleeves around the armhole, and the sleeves are then worked to the length desired.

Sizes:	S(M:L:XL:XXL)
Approx. measurements:	Chest: 97(107:117:127:137)cm / 38¼(42¼:46:50:54)in;
	Length: 66(68:71:74:76)cm / (26(26¾:28:29¼:30)in
Suggested yarns:	Sandnes Peer Gynt and Sandnes Børstet Alpakka
Yarn amount:	8(8:9:10:11) balls of 50g/91m/98yd Peer Gynt, DK
	(8-ply/light worsted) yarn; and 6(7:8:9:9) balls of
	50g/110m/120yd Børstet Alpakka, chunky (bulky) yarn
Tension:	12 sts to 10cm (4in) square over stocking (stockinette)
	st using 7mm (UK 2, US 10½/11) needles
Suggested needles:	7mm (UK 2, US 10½/11) circular needle and 6mm
	(UK 4, US 10) circular needle for rib and neck
Approx. length of zip:	23cm (9in)
Zip:	You can adapt the pattern to your chosen zip by a
	couple of centimetres (¾in) or so by making the neck
	higher or lower. It is not recommended to buy a zip that
	is a lot longer or shorter than the length stated.

Cast on 116(128:140:152:164) sts on a 6mm (UK 4, US 10) circular needle using 1 strand of each yarn together. Work 7 rounds of k1, p1 rib. Change to 7mm (UK 2, US 10½/11) needle and stocking (stockinette) st. Place one marker at start of round and one at the halfway point. These mark the sides of the sweater and where you will later divide for the armhole. Work until work measures 45(47:49:51:53)cm / 17¾(18½:19¾:20¾:21¼)in. Cast (bind) off 4 sts at each side, 2 before and 2 after marker.

Front: work back and forth across front until work measures 50(52:55:58:60)cm / 19¾(20½:21¾:22¾:23½)in. Place marker at centre front, where the zip will be inserted.

Left front: On next RS row, knit until 7 sts before marker. Work these sts in p1, k1 rib and end with k1 (edge st) before marker. Turn and work in patt as set back the other way. Rep until work measures 62(64:66:68:70)cm / 24½(25¼:26:26¾:27½)in. Place the 7 sts at the neck, the rib sts, onto a st holder or waste yarn. Continue to work back and forth in stocking (stockinette) st. At the same time: on each RS row, knit to last 2 sts before neck edge, k2tog. Rep 4(5:5:6:6) times in total. Work back and forth across rem sts until work measures 66(68:71:74:76)cm / 26(26¾:28:29¼:30)in. Break yarn. Leave sts on needle or move to a st holder or thread.

Continued overleaf.

Right front: starting at armhole, purl until 7 sts before marker. Work these sts in k1, p1 rib and end with k1 (edge st) before marker. Turn and work in patt as set back the other way. Rep until work measures 62(64:66:68:70)cm / 24½(25¼:26:26¾:27½)in. Place the 7 sts at the neck, the rib sts, onto a st holder or waste yarn. Continue to work back and forth in stocking (stockinette) st. At the same time, on each WS row, purl to last 2 sts before neck edge, p2tog. Rep 4(5:5:6:6) times in total. Work back and forth across rem sts until work measures 66(68:71:74:76)cm / 26(26¾:28:29¼:30)in. Break yarn. Leave sts on needle or move to a st holder or waste yarn.

Back: work back and forth in stocking (stockinette) st until work measures 67(69:72:75:77)cm / 26½(27¼:28¼:29½:30¼)in, i.e. 1cm (½in) longer than the front. Graft sts on fronts to same number of sts on each side of back, or cast (bind) off and sew together at shoulders. Leave rem sts for neck on needle.

Neckband: knit sts for right front from holder/waste yarn onto a 6mm (UK 4, US 10) needle in rib patt as set. Pick up sts along neck edge. Knit neck sts onto needle in stocking (stockinette) st. Pick up same number of sts along other side of neck. Knit sts on holder for left front onto needle in patt as set. 59(63:63:67:67) sts. Work back and forth in rib patt as set on front edges and continue rib patt round whole neck. Work back and forth in rib until neckband measures 26cm (10¼in) measured from back. Here you can knit the neck longer or shorter to fit your chosen zip. Remember that the neckband will be doubled over and check against the zip to make sure it will fit. Cast (bind) off loosely. Check as you cast (bind) off that the edges are stretchy enough.

Zip: fold the neckband to the inside and stitch down, using one strand of chunky (bulky) yarn and a yarn needle. Start approx. 1cm (½in) in on each side to make room for the zip afterwards. Then insert the zip between the layers of the neck on each side, and down the inside of the opening. It should not go all the way up to the edge. Make sure you are happy with the zip placement. Pin so that the zip is sitting well and is even on both sides. Sew zip in by hand using 1 strand of Børstet Alpakka. The sts should be sewn inside the edge st and run all the way to the top and bottom of the zip for the best result.

Sleeves: pick up approx. 12 sts per 10cm (4in) around armhole. 54(54:58:62:62) sts. Work in the round in stocking (stockinette) st and place a marker at centre underarm on round 1. At the same time, k2tog after first st and k2tog before last st at each side of marker on every 8 rounds. Work until sleeve measures 45(46:47:48:49)cm / 17¾(18:18½:19¼:19¾)in or to desired length and dec to 24(26:26:28:28) sts. Change to 6mm (UK 4, US 10) needle and work 7 rounds in k1, p1 rib. Cast (bind) off in rib. Rep for other sleeve.

Weave in all loose ends.

#urbanpolargenser #urbanpolarsweater #witredesign

CHUNKY CARDIGAN

The chunky cardigan is a soft, warm cardigan, knitted using two strands of chunky (bulky) yarn on large needles. The rib button bands are worked at the end using one strand of yarn on smaller needles for a neat finish. The fit of the cardigan is quite wide, with pockets, a deep V-neck and stylishly low buttons at the front. It is knitted from the bottom up and stitches are picked up for the sleeves around the armhole and worked down to the length desired.

Sizes:	XS(S:M:L:XL)
Approx. measurements:	Chest: 102(112:122:132:142)cm / 40¼(44:48:52:56)in; Length: 57(60:63:66:69)cm / 22½(23½:23¾:26:27¼)in
Suggested yarn:	Rauma Puno
Yarn amount:	10(11:13:15:17) balls of 50g/110m/120yd Rauma Puno, chunky (bulky) yarn
Tension:	10 sts to 10cm (4in) in stocking (stockinette) st on a 10mm (UK 000, US 15) needle; 20 sts to 10cm (4in) on a 4.5mm (UK 7, US 7) needle
Suggested needles:	10mm (UK 000, US 15) circular needles (one extra); extra-long 4.5mm (UK 7, US 7) circular needles
Extras:	Four buttons

Cast on 98(108:118:128:138) sts using 2 strands of yarn on 10mm (UK 000, US 15) needles, place a marker after 24(27:29:32:34) sts and one the same number of sts before end of row. Work back and forth in stocking (stockinette) st until work measures 20(22:24:26:28)cm / 7¾(8¾:9½:10¼:11)in. You are now going to work the pockets.

On next RS row, knit 9(9:10:11:11) sts. Place a marker here and another marker after 10 sts. Use another 10mm (UK 000, US 15) needle to work these 10 sts back and forth in stocking (stockinette) st until pocket measures 30cm (11¾in). Knit the 10 sts back onto the original circular needle. The pocket will then fold itself in half inside the cardigan and will not be visible from the outside. Cont working cardigan and stop 19(19:20:21:21) sts before end of row. Place a marker here and another marker after 10 sts. Make this pocket in the same way as described above.

Cont working across whole cardigan until work measures 28(30:32:34:36)cm / 11(11¾:12½:13½:14¼)in. Now start to slant for the V-neck. Starting with a RS row, *k1, k2tog. Purl back to last 3 sts, k2tog tbl, k1. Purl back the other way. Rep decreases on every alt RS row, i.e. on every fourth row.*

When work measures 38(40:42:44:46)cm / 15(15¾:16½:17¼:18)in, dec 4 sts at each underarm, 2 before and 2 after the markers at the sides.

Left side of front: cont to dec as between * and * for neck 10(11:11:12:12) times in total, including decreases from before armhole. Work back and forth until work measures 57(60:63:66:69)cm / 22½(23½:24¾:26:27¼)in. Place sts on a st holder or waste yarn.

Right side of front: start at the armhole. On next RS row, cont to dec as between * and * for neck 10(11:11:12:12) times in total, including decreases from before armhole. Work back and forth until work measures 57(60:63:66:69)cm / 22½(23½:24¾:26:27¼)in. Place sts on a st holder or waste yarn.

Continued overleaf.

Back: work back and forth for back until back measures 1cm (½in) longer than the front. Graft sts on fronts to same number of sts on each side of back. Leave rem sts for neck on needle.

Button band: for best results, work entire band in one using an extra-long circular needle, or by joining the cables together. Otherwise, the different bands can be worked separately and sewn together at the end. If you choose to work the bands separately, avoid joins in highly visible places. It is important to pick up sts evenly around the edges so be sure to use a tape measure.

Start at bottom of right side and pick up approx. 15 sts per 10cm (4in) using a single strand of yarn on an extra-long, 4.5mm (UK 7, US 7) needle. Knit sts at neck onto needle working into both front and back legs of st for a firm join. Pick up the same number of sts down left side. Turn and work back and forth in rib as foll: p1 (edge st), p1, k1 and end with p1, p1 (edge st). Adapt number of sts on first needle to make rib work. Continue to work back and forth in rib until band measures 4cm (1½in).

Place work flat on a table and place markers where you want buttonholes. On next row, cast (bind) off 2 sts at each marker. On next row, cast on 2 new sts at each marker. Work until band measures 6cm (2½in) and work one purl row to mark fold line. Work another 5.5cm (1¾in) and work buttonholes again so that they will be in the same place on this side when the band is folded over to the inside. Knit edge down and cast (bind) off. Sew around the buttonholes with yarn to produce an even, sturdy edge.

Sleeves: starting at underarm, pick up 36(40:44:48:52) sts using 2 strands of yarn on a 10mm (UK 000, US 15) circular needle. Place a marker at centre underarm to mark start of round. Work sleeve in stocking (stockinette) st in the round, and k2tog before and after the marker every 7cm (2¾in) five times in total. Work until sleeve measures 45cm (17¾in) or to desired length. Break off 1 strand of yarn and change to 4.5mm (UK 7, US 7) circular needles. Work in the round in k1, p1 rib, and dec to approx. 26(28:30:32:34) sts on round 1. Cont until rib measures 10cm (4in). Cast (bind) off loosely in rib.

Sew edges of both pockets together. Weave in all loose ends. Press hem of cardigan well so the edge lies flat and does not roll up.

#grovrøkejakke #chunkycardigan #witredesign

> **Tips**
> • *All bodies are different. It is a good idea to measure the knitting against the wearer as you go along.*
> • *Remember to check your tension.*
> • *Knit the hem down as you go. For more information, Search for 'cast-off hem for top-down knitting' (or 'knit a folded hem') videos online.*
> • *The cardigan is grafted together at the shoulders. Search for videos on 'grafting stocking (stockinette) stitch' or 'Kitchener stitch' online.*

SNUG TURTLENECK

The snug turtleneck is a oversized, cropped sweater worked using three strands of mohair yarn. It is light to wear and hangs well, while being cozy and warm at the same time. The neckband is folded over and sewn down on the inside, making it stand up nicely and fit snugly. Apart from this one seam, there is no other assembly involved. The sweater is knitted from the bottom up and front and back sections are grafted together at the shoulders. Stitches are then picked up for the sleeves, which are knitted from the top down, to the desired length. The sleeves are slightly narrow, which looks good with the slightly oversized design for the body.

Sizes:	XS(S:M:L:XL)
Approx. measurements:	Chest: 104(114:124:134:144)cm / 41(44¾:48¾:52¾:56¾)in;
	Length: 43(46:49:52:55)cm / 17(18:19¾:20½:21¾)in
Suggested yarn:	Hip Mohair
Yarn amount:	10(11:13:15:17) balls of 25g/210m/230yd balls of Hip Mohair, 1–3-ply
	(lace weight) yarn
Tension:	14 sts to 10cm (4in) square in stocking (stockinette) st using 6mm (UK 4,
	US 10) needles
Suggested needles:	6mm (UK 4, US 10) circular needle; short 4mm (UK 8, US 6) circular needle
	for neckband

Cast on 136(150:164:178:192) sts using 3 strands of yarn on a 6mm (UK 4, US 10) circular needle. Work 5 rounds of k1, p1 rib in the round. Change to stocking (stockinette) st and on round 1, inc 10 sts. 146(160:174:188:202) sts. Place a marker at start of round and another after 73(80:87:94:101) sts. Cont in stocking (stockinette) st until work measures 25(27:29:31:33)cm / 9¾(10¾:11½:12¼:13)in. Cast (bind) off 4 sts at each side, 2 before and 2 after each side marker. You now have 69(76:83:90:97) sts for front and for back.

Front: work back and forth across front until work measures 37(40:43:46:49)cm / 14½(15¾:17:18:19¾)in. On next RS row, place centre 15(16:17:18:19) sts for neck on a st holder or waste yarn. These sts can also be cast (bound) off but will need to be picked up again for the neckband.

Right side of front: knit to end of row. Turn, purl back until last 2 sts before neck, k2tog. Turn, k2tog at start of next row and cont to armhole. Rep decreases on every row at neck edge six times in total. Cont in stocking (stockinette) st until work measures 43(46:49:52:55)cm / 17(18:19¾:20½:21¾)in. Place sts on a st holder or waste yarn.

Left side of front: starting at the armhole, knit to last 2 sts before neck edge, k2tog. Turn, k2tog at start of next row. Rep decreases on every row at neck edge six times in total. Cont in stocking (stockinette) st until work measures 43(46:49:52:55)cm / 17(18:19¾:20½:21¾)in. Place sts on a st holder or waste yarn.

Back: work back and forth until work measures 44(47:50:53:56)cm / 17¼(18½:19¾:20¾:22)in, i.e. 1cm (½in) longer than the front. Graft sts on fronts to same number of sts on each side of back. Leave rem sts for neck on needle.

Neckband: place neck sts on a 4mm (UK 8, US 6) needle and pick up sts along neck edge down towards front. Knit sts from front neck onto the needle in stocking (stockinette) st and pick up the same number of sts along other side of neck. Pick up enough sts to make the neck even, without holes. Work in the round in k1, p1 rib, and dec to approx. 64(64:68:68:72) sts on first rounds.

Work in the round in rib until neckband measures 20cm (7¾in). Cast (bind) off loosely, remembering to check your head fits through the neckband.

Sleeves: pick up 48(48:50:52:54) sts around armhole on a 6mm (UK 4, US 10) circular needle and place marker at centre underarm. Cont in stocking (stockinette) st in the round. At the same time, k2tog after first st and k2tog before last st at each side of marker on every 5 rounds, six times in total. Work sleeve to desired length, approx. 44(44:46:48:48)cm / 17¼(17¼:18:19:19)in. Dec to 28(30:30:32:32) sts on next round. Switch to rib: k1, p1. Repeat rib pattern for five rounds in total. Cast (bind) off in rib. Rep for other sleeve.

Weave in all loose ends. Fold over neckband to the inside and sew down with a yarn needle and one strand of yarn.

#lunturtleneck
#snugturtleneck
#witredesign

Tips
• *All bodies are different. It is a good idea to measure the knitting against the wearer as you go along.*
• *Remember to check your tension.*
• *The sweater is grafted together at the shoulders. Search for videos online on 'grafting stocking (stockinette) stitch' or 'Kitchener stitch'.*
• *If you are knitting a size where the number of balls is not divisible by three, use both the outside strand and the inside strand from one of the balls, either for the whole work or only at the end.*

MUSKOX JACKET

The muskox jacket is a thick, warm jacket in brioche stitch, which can easily be worn as a coat. It is knitted from the bottom up, dividing for the front and back before grafting them together at the shoulders. Stitches are then picked up around the armholes and the sleeves are knitted from the top down, to the desired length. The jacket has an i-cord cast-(bind-)off at the neck, the cuffs and the waist, which looks great and adds an extra design feature.

Sizes:	Age 1–2(3–4:5–6:7–8:9–10)
Approx. measurements:	Chest: 72(77:81:86:90)cm / 28¼(30¼:32:33¾:35½)in;
	Length: 35(37:39:42:45)cm / (13¾(14½:15¼16½:17¾)in
Suggested yarn:	Hip Wool
Yarn amount:	7(9:11:13:16) balls of 50g/80m/87yd balls of Hip Wool,
	aran (10-ply/worsted) yarn
Tension:	9 sts to 10cm (4in) in brioche st
Suggested needles:	7mm (UK 2, US 10½/11) circular needle

Cast on 65(69:73:77:81) sts using 2 strands of yarn on a 7mm (UK 2, US 10½/11) circular needle.

Set-up row: k1 (edge st), *k1, yfwd, sl1 loosely purlwise*. Rep from * to *. End with k1 + k1 (edge st). Row 2: k1 (edge st). * yfwd, sl1 loosely purlwise. Knit next st and yfwd together*. Rep from * to *. End with yfwd, s1 loosely purlwise + k1 (edge st). Row 3: k1 (edge st). *Knit next st and yfwd together; yfwd, loosely sl1 purlwise*. Rep from * to *. End by knitting next st and yfwd together + k1 (edge st). Rep rows 2 and 3 until work measures 23(25:26:28:30)cm / 9(9¾:10¼:11:11¾)n. On next RS row, work 17(17:19:19:21) sts, k2tog. Work until last 18(18:20:20:22) sts, k2tog. Knit to end of row.

Left front: turn and work the 17(17:19:19:21) sts until work measures 32(34:36:39:42)cm / 12½(13½:14¼15¼:16½)in. The last st before armhole is now an edge st and must be worked as a knit st on every row.

Neckband: on next WS row start with k2tog. Rep dec on every WS row 3(4:5:6:7) times in total and cont in brioche st until work measures 35(37:39:42:45)cm / 13¾(14½:15¼:16½:17¾)in. Place rem sts on a st holder or waste yarn.

Back: work back to same length as front. The first and last sts of the row are now edge sts and must be worked as knit sts on every row.

Right front: start at armhole and work over rem sts until work measures 32(34:36:39:44)cm / 12½(13½:14¼:15¼:17¼)in. The last st before armhole is now an edge st and must be knitted on every row.

Neckband: on next RS row, start by k2tog. Rep dec on every RS row 3(4:5:6:7) times in total and cont until work measures 35(37:39:42:45)cm / 13¾(14½:15¼:16½:17¾)in.

Graft sts on back and front together, or cast (bind) off and sew together at shoulders. Leave rem sts for neck on a st holder.

Continued on page 194.

Button bands: pick up sts along right front, approx. 11 sts to 10cm (4in). Work 4 rows in stocking (stockinette) st. Cast (bind) off.

Pick up same number of sts along left front. Work 2 rows in stocking (stockinette) st. Make buttonholes where you want them; sl1, k2tog. Work 1 row in stocking (stockinette) st = 4 rows in total. Cast (bind) off.

i-cord cast-(bind-)off at neck: start above right button band and pick up st at top of band and along neck edge, knit sts for neck onto needle and pick up same number of sts down and across button band on left side. 35(40:45:50:55) sts. Cast on 2 new sts at end of row.

Turn and work as foll: k1, slip next 2 sts loosely one by one, place them back on left-hand needle and k2tog tbl. Slip the 2 sts on right-hand needle back onto left-hand needle. Rep until 2 sts rem on needle, k2tog.

Sleeves: start at bottom of sleeve and pick up 25(27:29:33:37) sts inside edge st. Rep the set-up row and rows 2 and 3 at the start of the instructions. Work back and forth, and at the same time k2tog for the two first and two last sts of the row every 7cm (2¾in), 1(1:2:2:3) times in total.

Work until sleeve measures 16(20:24:28:32)cm (6¼(7¾:9½:11:12½)in. On next RS row dec to 14(17:20:23:26) sts. Cast on 2 new sts at end of row. Turn and work i-cord cast off as for neck.

Rep for other sleeve.

i-cord hem: start at left side of jacket and pick up 1 st in every st along the edge. Cast on 2 new sts at end of round. Turn and work i-cord cast off as described for the neck.

Sew up sleeves. Weave in all loose ends and sew on buttons.

#moskusjakka #muskoxjacket #witredesign

Tips
• *All bodies are different. It is a good idea to measure the knitting against the wearer as you go along.*
• *Remember to check your tension. If your tension is too tight, you will use more yarn.*
• *Brioche stitch can be tricky to measure. Place the garment flat and leave it for a while to rest before measuring.*
• *The yarn forward and the stitch it is knitted with are counted as one stitch throughout.*
• *The jacket can be rinsed, dried flat and slightly stretched while damp. This helps the stitches to 'settle' at the right length. Make sure the sleeves do not get too long.*
• *If you are brave enough, you can gently felt it. The technique works well with this jacket.*

TIPS

There is a 'Tips' section in every pattern. Read this before you start. And remember that the internet is your best friend for learning new things, including knitting skills. Search for and watch great videos by skilled knitters who will show you what to do. This book features several patterns with a 'raw' edge, such as the Nordic summer top (see page 130). To make these garments look their best, it is important to work edge sts as knit sts. The instructions will tell you to always knit the last st in the row, and then to slip the first st of the next row loosely off the needle with the yarn to the front.

Like clothes in the shop, not every knitting pattern will hit the mark with everyone. Your own figure, style and taste are important in getting a result you are happy with. Making your own clothes means you can modify the fit as you go along, ending up with clothes that are perfect for you or your wearer. Always measure and try on as you go.

Knitting is the opposite of fast fashion; it is slow fashion. It is meant to take its time and the things you make will enjoy a good, long lifetime, without a huge environmental footprint.

Remember to *enjoy it*!

Share your own creations from this book on social media using the hashtag #witredesign and the hashtags after every pattern.

THANK YOUS

A big thank you to everyone who has test-knitted the patterns and knitted model versions for a whole year, and managed to keep the book a secret. You have been part of bringing all the threads together. It has been a true joy to have you as part of the team.

Marit Nybakke Islann, Mari Torsholt and Dina Fonn Sætre – I'm really happy you wanted to be with me in the cafe in Frogner Park, and go out to Sørenga and light a bonfire on the island of Engeløya. Thanks for being models for the book.

Lars, Mikkel, Pelle and Otto <3 You have been part of the journey every day, and a bit extra on the days in the photos. Thanks for making me smile and laugh.

Thank you for coming round and producing amazing illustrations, Victoria Krekling! You helped take the book to a new level.

A Knitter's Year would probably not have been created if it hadn't been for photographer Helena Krekling. Our meeting, and her approach when she meets the people she is taking photos of, have been vital to the project. I'm incredibly proud of what we have accomplished. Thank you for wanting to be part of it.

KNITTING NEEDLE CONVERSION CHART

EUROPE/ METRIC (MM)	US	OLD UK SIZES
2	0	14
2.25	1	13
2.5	-	-
2.75	2	12
3	3	11
3.25	4	10
3.5	4	-
3.75	5	9
4	6	8
4.5	7	7
5	8	6
5.5	9	5
6	10	4
6.5	10½	3
7	-	2
7.5	-	1
8	11	0
9	13	00
10	15	000
12 or 13	17	-
15	20	-

First published in Great Britain 2023 by
Search Press Limited
Wellwood, North Farm Road,
Tunbridge Wells, Kent TN2 3DR

Originally published as: *Witre Design*
Copyright © Cappelen Dam, 2020

English translation by Burravoe Translation Services

Photography: Helena Krekling
Design and layout: Ingrid Skjæraasen
Repro: Narayana Press, Denmark

ISBN: 978-1-80092-105-4
ebook ISBN: 978-1-80093-096-4

Suppliers
If you have difficulty in obtaining any of the materials and equipment mentioned in this book, then please visit the Search Press website for details of suppliers:
www.searchpress.com

You are invited to visit the author's website: www.witredesign.no/en/